PLANET EARTH

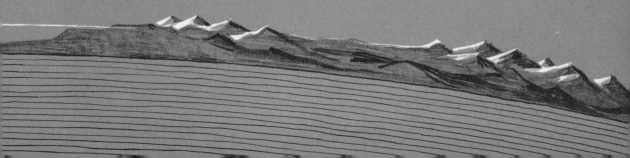

Where did the earth come from? What is it made of? Why does it have continents? In what ways does the sun affect our planet?

Scientists have long sought answers to these and other important questions about the planet Earth. Today, with rockets and satellites and deep-sea drills, with electronic eyes and ears, scientists have the means of discovering the earth's big secrets.

In this absorbing book, Patricia Lauber tells of the great new age of exploration that began with the International Geophysical Year—in space, under the oceans, and into the depths of the earth itself.

In a previous book, **All About the Planets** (praised by experts as "the best book on the subject for this age group"), Miss Lauber skillfully conveyed an understanding of our solar system as a whole. Now, in this book, she shows how much and how little we know about our home—the planet Earth.

All About the Planet Earth

All About The Planet Earth

by

PATRICIA LAUBER

ILLUSTRATED WITH DRAWINGS BY

LEE J. AMES

AND WITH PHOTOGRAPHS

allabout books

RANDOM HOUSE · NEW YORK

PHOTOGRAPH CREDITS: Dr. George Bell, page 50; Boyden Station of Harvard College Observatory, Bloemfontein, South Africa, 73; Free Lance Photographers Guild, 8-9, 78-79; Gardner Collection, Harvard University, 52-53; General Mills, Inc., 89; Harvard Radio Astronomy Station, Fort Davis, Texas, 130; Vic Hessler, University of Alaska, 126; High Altitude Observatory, University of Colorado, Boulder, Colorado, 114; Lamont Geological Observatory, 5; Monkmeyer Press Photo Service, 29; Mount Wilson and Palomar Observatories, 111; National Academy of Sciences, 88, 93; National Aeronautics and Space Administration, 136; National Science Foundation, 58, 59; Royal Canadian Air Force, 104; Dr. Martin Schwarzschild, Princeton University Observatory, 112; Soviet Geophysical Committee, Academy of Sciences of the USSR, 134; State University of Iowa, 122; Three Lions, 12; Underwood and Underwood, 16; U.S. Navy, 67; Woods Hole Oceanographic Institution, 62, 95.

By permission of Alfred A. Knopf, Inc., the drawing on page 64 is adapted from a diagram by Alex Aiken in *IGY: The Year of the New Moon* by J. Tuzo Wilson.

To Dr. Maurice Ewing, Director of the Lamont Geological Observatory, the author and the publisher are grateful for his careful review of the text of this book. To Dr. Charles Drake, assistant professor of geology, Columbia University, they are grateful for his helpful suggestions about the illustrations.

Design by Paul Bacon Studio

Contents

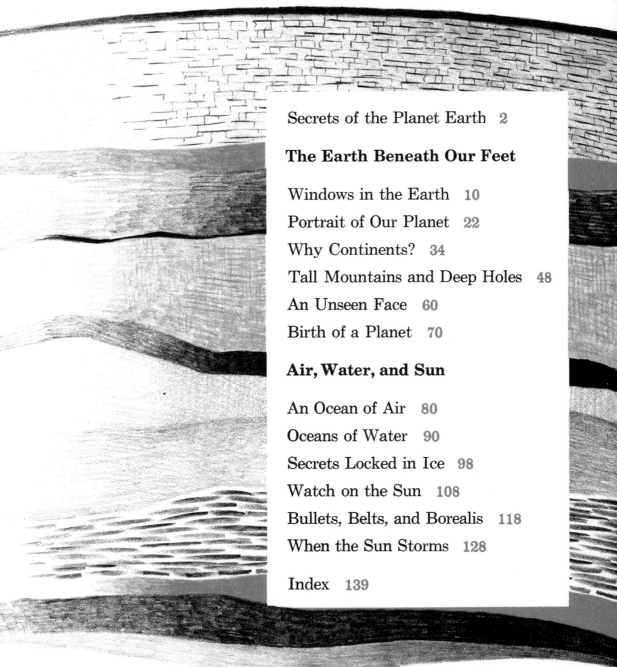

All About the Planet Earth

Secrets
of the
Planet
Earth

Nearly 500 years ago a great age of discovery began. In small ships of sail, men set out to explore the earth.

The task was as big as the earth itself. And so for generations men sailed seas, charted mountains, traced rivers, and measured plains. They hacked trails through jungles. They battled the ice and winds of polar wastes.

At last, in this century, the task was done. Where men could go, men had gone. Their journeys were described in books. Their findings filled fat atlases for all to see.

Yet, in a sense, men had only begun to explore the earth. They had mapped only the features of its face. In every other way, the unknowns far outnumbered the knowns.

A great new age of exploration began with the IGY.

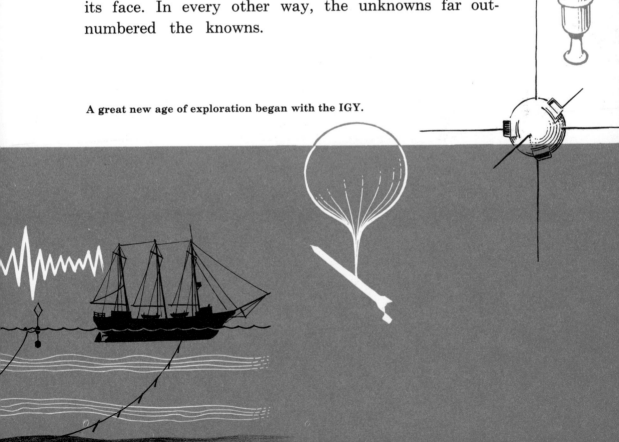

Today we live in a great new age of exploration. This is scientific exploration, designed to pry loose the deepest secrets of our planet. And it moves in realms never dreamed of by explorers of old—in space, under the oceans, and into the depths of the earth itself.

This new age of exploration started with the International Geophysical Year, running from July 1, 1957, through December 31, 1958. During the IGY more than 60,000 scientists from 66 countries launched a mass attack on the unknowns of the earth.

By boat and plane, by snow tractor, and on foot, the scientists fanned out. They set up 4,000 major scientific stations on everything from the Andes Mountains to ice islands adrift in the Arctic Ocean. Where they could not go themselves, they sent electronic eyes and ears.

Measuring, observing, testing, probing, IGY scientists piled up huge heaps of facts and figures. And when they began to sift these findings, even scientists were surprised to learn how little we know about our home, the earth.

Beneath the oceans lies a rugged, unseen landscape. Here are mountains taller than Everest. Here is a chasm deep enough to swallow seven Grand Canyons. Here, too, is a submarine mountain range that circles the earth.

Under its giant icecap, Antarctica is a fifth smaller than anyone had thought.

Maurice Ewing, a leading earth scientist, prepares to lower a coring apparatus from a research vessel to the ocean bottom.

Mighty forces within the earth are changing familiar places. New land is rising in the Caribbean, the Gulf of California, and the Red Sea. In some future age California may split away from the continental United States. The Hawaiian Islands lie in an area where some great force is—very, very slowly—thrusting up new islands at one end of the chain, while older ones behind tend to sink. And so the Hawaiian Islands may, in some distant time, sink into the sea.

Unexpectedly, the earth has turned out to be slightly pear-shaped. Just as unexpected—a vast belt of atomic particles encircles the earth, trapped by our planet's magnetic field.

The task now facing scientist-explorers is to fit these discoveries into a kind of giant jigsaw puzzle. Assembled, the puzzle will show a portrait of the planet Earth. But the puzzle is far from being complete. Many of the pieces are still missing. Others cannot yet be fitted in, for scientists do not have "a picture on the box" to guide them. Instead, they must build theories and test them against the known facts.

Their task is a tremendous one, pulling together the many fields called the earth sciences. It is also difficult, because the earth is hard to study. There is as yet no way scientists can back off into space and observe the earth as it whirls in its ancient orbit around the sun. There is no way they can cut out a section and study the earth from the crust beneath our feet to the central core. There is no way they can look back through the 4.5 billion years of the earth's history to see its birth.

Yet, little by little, scientists are piecing together the puzzle. They are beginning to understand how the sun affects the earth. They are beginning to understand the working relationship of the waters, winds, and heat that make our weather. And they are coming close to learning why the earth has continents; why it has mountains; whether the continents drift; what lies under the crust; what causes volcanoes and earthquakes. They are coming close to learning what unseen forces shape and change this not-so-solid earth.

This book is a brief introduction to the work of modern scientific explorers. It is a sampler of problems, of questions without answers, and of challenges that face those who seek the secrets of the planet Earth.

The Earth Beneath Our Feet

Windows
in the
Earth

February 20, 1943, began like any other day for a Mexican farmer named Dionisio Polido. He rose before dawn, ate breakfast, and set out for the cornfield he was planning to work. Almost immediately he discovered that this day was strangely different.

The ground felt hot beneath his bare feet, though the sun had not had time to warm it.

Several times he thought he heard thunder, but the sky was clear with not a cloud in sight.

Then Polido arrived at his cornfield and saw a column of smoke rising from the far end. Thinking that something had caught fire, he hurried over to beat out the flames. But the smoke was not coming from a fire. Instead, Polido saw that the very ground had cracked open and a smoking, gray-white material was bubbling out of the crack.

Polido fled—surely the world was coming to an end! But, as he later learned, what he had seen was the birth of a volcano. Its name is Parícutin.

This cross section shows the inside of one kind of volcano. Its cone was built as molten rock forced its way through the earth's crust in eruptions. At first, magma traveled the center vent or throat. When this vent was blocked by a column of hardened lava, magma probed for weak places and forced its way into them.

In the days following its birth, Parícutin erupted with enormous violence. The opening in the cornfield grew into a long crack with a pear-shaped hole at one end. Smoke, sparks, and ashlike dust billowed out of the crack. Glowing rocks the size of automobiles were hurled from the hole. Parícutin poured forth so much lava and ash that in only five days' time it built a 300-foot-high cone above the original hole. In a matter of weeks, lava oozing from a great crack in the ground had advanced over a mile of land. It swallowed the Polido farm. Farther on, it swallowed two villages, burying them so deep that only the church steeples remained in sight. All the people who had farmed and lived in the area were moved away.

By the time Parícutin was a year old, it stood 1,410 feet high. Then its growth began to slow. When the eruptions stopped on February 25, 1952, the volcano was 1,500 feet tall.

During its birth and growth Parícutin was studied closely by a number of scientists. They had never before had a chance to watch a volcano grow from a hole in the ground to a height of 1,500 feet. And scientists are very interested in volcanoes for two main reasons.

The first is that they are trying to learn what causes volcanoes. So far they have not discovered the basic cause, but they can explain in part what happens. Great pockets of molten rock called magma lie under certain parts of the earth's crust. When

13

Parícutin, volcano born in a cornfield in 1943.

magma finds a crack in the rock of the crust, it forces its way to the surface and bursts out as smoke, gas, dust, and lava. This is what happened in Polido's cornfield.

No one knows just how, why, or where magma forms inside the earth. Nor does anyone know exactly what it is made of; since magma separates into dust, gas, and lava as it erupts, no one has ever been able to take a sample of it. But scientists do know that magma is molten rock that contains several gases in solution. The two chief gases are steam and carbon dioxide.

Gas makes the molten rock lively, much as gas makes soda pop lively. If you shake a capped soda bottle, nothing happens because the pressure is contained. But if you then remove the cap, a small explosion takes place. With the pressure released, the carbon dioxide of the bubbles suddenly expands, carrying the liquid with it, and the soda pop shoots out of the bottle.

When magma finds an opening, its gases expand violently, widening the crack in the crust. Then, with the way out charted, a red-hot column of magma blasts its way to the surface. Sometimes the explosion is so great that the magma's solid material is turned into a powdery ash. Sometimes the gases escape more slowly. Then the material they are carrying oozes out of the earth. The material left, after the gases have escaped, is lava.

Once the pressure in the magma is reduced, the

volcano stops erupting. Sometimes the pressure never builds up again, and the volcano sleeps forever. Sometimes, after sleeping for years, a volcano again stirs with life. Pressure once more builds up in the magma and the magma once more seeks an opening. Then the volcano may erupt with enormous violence. That was what happened with Mount Pelée in the French West Indies. Early in the morning of May 8, 1902, magma blasted a big new crater, ripping out the side of the mountain. A great wave of steam and fiery gas rolled over the city of St. Pierre, killing 40,000 people in a matter of minutes. Fire turned the buildings into charred ruins.

Still other volcanoes, such as Hawaii's Moana Loa, are not violent. Rising 28,000 feet from the bottom of the Pacific, Moana Loa has been built by countless small flows of lava, rather than by violent eruptions. Because Moana Loa is not dangerous, scientists can study it from an observatory built on the volcano's slopes.

Here scientists have learned the symptoms that precede an eruption—a swarm of small earthquakes, deep thunder-like rumblings, and a swelling of the ground as magma wells up. Here they have taken samples of the gases and lava that boil out of a crater. Here they have measured the temperature of erupting lava.

The sampling and measurements give scientists what little direct evidence they have about the inside of the earth. And that is the second reason why

15

Ruins of St. Pierre, photographed shortly after the 1902 eruption of Mount Pelée.

they are interested in volcanoes. Volcanoes are windows in the earth. They are one of the few ways scientists can "see" into the earth beneath our feet. And, as you will learn later, volcanoes have provided important information about our planet.

A second window in the earth is the study of gravity.

As scientists discovered some 250 years ago, the pull of gravity is not the same in every part of the earth. Two things affect it. One is distance from the center of the earth. The second is the density of material in the place where gravity is being measured.

The discovery that gravity varies gave scientists a tool for exploring the earth. Gravity measurements provided the first clue that the earth has a crust which lies on a different, more dense material, called the mantle. Gravity measurements have shown that the earth is not perfectly round.

Most information about the inside of the earth, however, has come from the study of earthquake waves. They are a third window in the earth.

Every year this not-so-solid earth is shaken by at least ten major earthquakes and perhaps a million smaller ones. All these quakes, big and small, are symptoms of movement within our planet.

The basic cause of an earthquake is an unknown force—or forces—within the earth. This force puts rocks of the crust and the upper mantle under severe strain. If the force builds up very slowly, the rocks simply flow or bend, for they are slightly elastic. But if it suddenly increases, the rock breaks—or, as geologists say, it faults. With the break, the rock snaps straight and vibrates. Great vibrations, or shock waves, are sent shooting through the earth. This is an earthquake. And it can be one of the most terrifying experiences known to man. For example:

On the bright frosty morning of December 4, 1957, a man named Sangidorzh was riding his camel along the foot of a mountain in Mongolia. Suddenly man and camel were hurled to the ground and stunned. The tops of two mountains tumbled into a valley and piled up 1,100 feet high. A dammed-up river cut through a mountain and broke out on the other side as a waterfall. Huge boulders popped out of the mountainsides and bowled into the valleys. With a dreadful sound, the ground cracked open into two great faults, 150 and 100 miles long. A major earthquake had taken place.

An earthquake can also occur along an existing fault, when pressure forces the two surfaces of rock to slip past each other. That was the cause of the famous 1906 earthquake that hit San Francisco.

The center of the quake was the San Andreas Fault, a great crack in the earth that runs for 600 miles across California's coastal ranges of mountains. For many years the fault had been quiet. The two surfaces had pressed together without causing any motion. Then, during the 1800's, forces within the

18

earth strained the fault, shoving, twisting, and bending its rock. The pressures grew and grew until, on

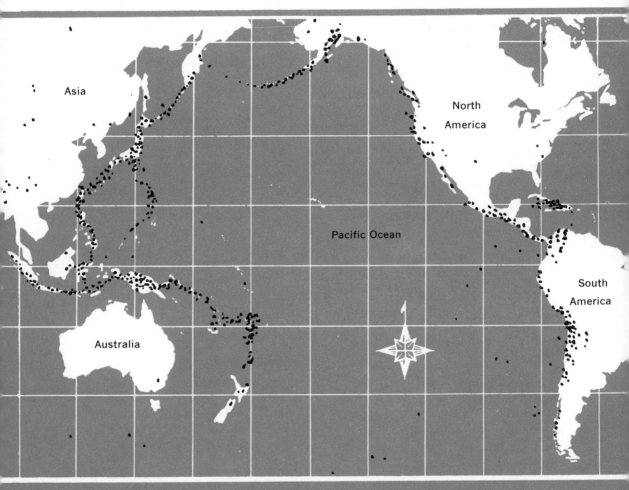

Most of the earth's active volcanoes lie on the rim of the Pacific Ocean basin.
Most earthquakes also occur here. But no one yet knows why volcanoes and
earthquakes should occur in the same region.

19

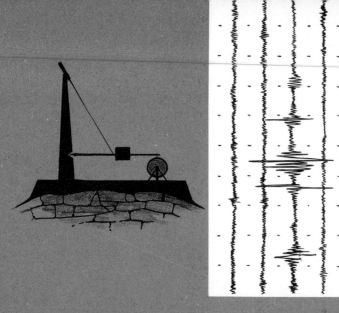

Sensitive instruments called seismographs (left) record the tremors (center) caused by earthquakes. By comparing records made in different areas, scientists can plot the paths taken by earthquake waves (below). Paths and speeds of the waves reveal much about the unseen interior of the earth.

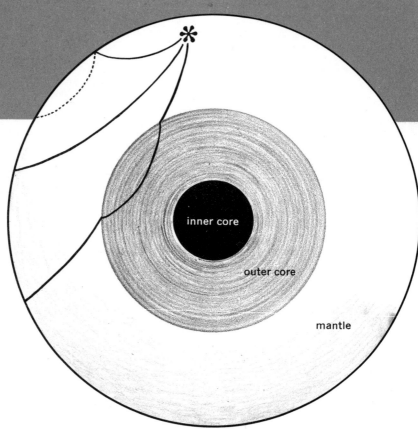

inner core

outer core

mantle

the morning of April 18, 1906, the fault snapped along a 270-mile section. As the pressure was released, shock waves shot out from the fault. Within a minute of the fault's snapping, surface waves had shaken San Francisco, twisting and cracking hundreds of buildings. Fire broke out and swept the city.

Surface waves from an earthquake do the damage. But waves that travel deep into the earth have proved one of the most valuable tools known to earth scientists.

Scientists who study earthquakes work chiefly in observatories. There sensitive instruments detect, measure, and record the passage of earthquake waves.

An earthquake sends out several different kinds of waves. The different kinds follow different paths in the earth. Some follow the hard crust. Others penetrate the earth for hundreds or thousands of miles before coming out.

In their journeys, the waves are affected by the kind of material they encounter. Their speeds change. Their paths may be bent. They may be reflected back. Some waves can pass through solids, liquids, or gases. Others can pass only through solids.

By studying what happens to earthquake waves, scientists have learned a great deal about the inside of the earth. They have gained a kind of X-ray picture of an earth we never see. This, together with their studies of volcanoes and gravity, has helped them sketch a portrait of our planet.

Portrait of Our Planet

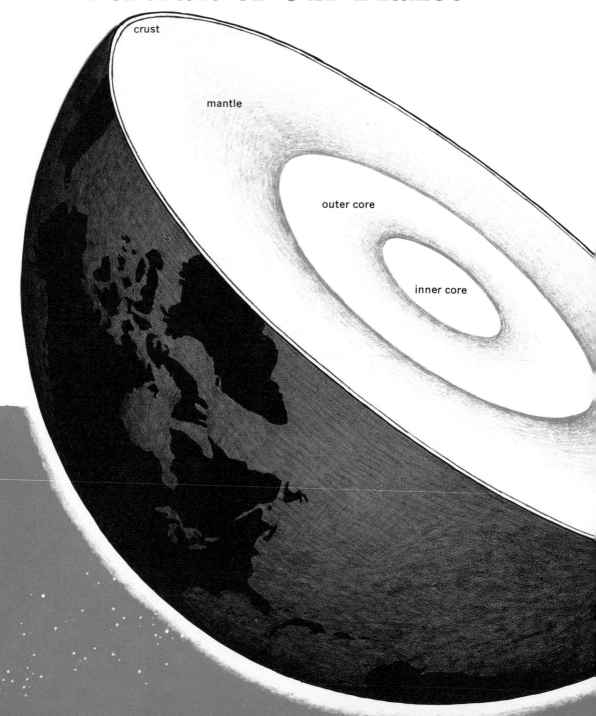

crust

mantle

outer core

inner core

A portrait of the earth painted in broad, bold strokes shows it as one of a family of planets circling the star we call our sun. Third planet out from the sun, the earth whirls around its orbit at 66,600 miles an hour. About 8,000 miles in diameter, the earth is a sphere of rock and metal, wrapped in an atmosphere several hundred miles thick.

The portrait is a great and remarkable one since no scientist has yet seen the earth as a planet. But scientists cannot be content with the bold strokes of an outline. They must fill in the rest of the portrait. And, just as a portrait painter must study bone and muscle structure, so scientists must study the shape and structure of the earth.

The general shape of the earth has been known for a very long time. Greek scientists discovered that the earth was round some 2500 years ago. Nearly 300 years ago, Isaac Newton suggested that the earth

We live on the earth's thin crust. It rests on the mantle, which accounts for about 85 per cent of the earth's volume.

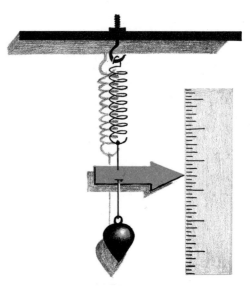

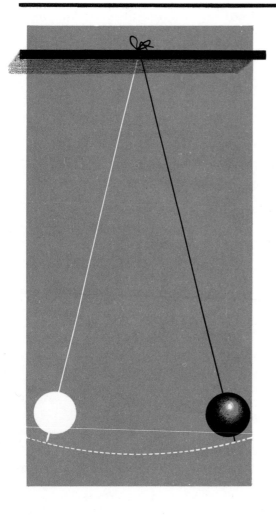

Before the age of satellites, scientists had only two devices for measuring the earth's gravity: the pendulum and the gravimeter. The gravimeter (above) is essentially a very sensitive scale that always weighs a standard mass. The weight of this mass varies with the pull of gravity. Where gravity is stronger, it weighs more. The pendulum (left) can be used because the downward part of each swing is a fall. And the rate of fall is determined by gravity.

was not, as most people thought, perfectly round. Newton believed that the earth's spinning must cause it to bulge at the equator and be flattened at the poles. Gravity measurements later proved him right. Gravity is stronger at the poles than at the equator because the poles are closer to the center of the earth. The earth's diameter, measured from pole to pole, is about 27 miles smaller than at the equator.

Scientists knew that this new picture of the earth was true, but they could not be sure it was complete. So they continued to study the earth by making gravity measurements. Progress was slow, for it involved moving over the whole surface of the earth, measuring here and measuring there. Then, during the IGY, scientists suddenly had a wonderful new tool: man-made satellites, orbiting the earth. Now they could measure gravity in terms of its effect on satellite orbits.

If gravity were the same all over the earth, a satellite's orbit would be perfectly regular. But gravity varies, depending on how the earth's mass is distributed. And variations in gravity affect a satellite's orbit. Where gravity is stronger, the satellite is pulled in toward the earth. Where gravity is weaker, the satellite swings away from the earth.

By painstaking study of satellite orbits, IGY scientists made an unexpected discovery: the earth is very slightly pear-shaped, being smaller in the north than in the south. Further study showed that the pear has bulges—a 45-foot one at the North Pole and a bulge of 1,400 feet at the part of the equator just off eastern Brazil.

These irregularities are very small. They are so small that they would not even show on a scale model the size of a classroom globe. Yet they are important because they involve huge amounts of material.

So far no one has managed to explain why the earth should be shaped like a bulging pear. The cause, it is thought, must lie hidden within the earth, probably in the region called the mantle.

The earth, as scientists have known for some time, has three main regions: the core, the mantle, and the crust. The core lies at the center of the earth. The mantle surrounds the core. And the rocky crust surrounds the mantle.

We live on the crust, but we see very little of it. In the long, long life of the earth, great layers of sediment have been laid down on the crust, as wind, rain, and frost pried loose tiny fragments of rock. However, the crust is the only region of the earth that scientists can readily reach. And they have learned that it is made of two main kinds of rock.

The continents are made of granite, a relatively light rock. Continental crust is 22 to 37 miles thick. The crust beneath the oceans is much thinner—only 3 to 3½ miles thick. It is made of basalt, a much denser rock than granite. Why the crust should be made of two very different kinds of rock is one of the big unanswered questions facing earth scientists.

The boundary where crust ends and mantle begins was discovered in 1909 by a Yugoslav scientist named Andrija Mohorovičić. Since the boundary is named for him, scientists have dubbed it the Moho. Above the Moho is the crust. Below it is the mantle. At the Moho the velocity of earthquake waves suddenly changes as they enter the denser mantle.

The mantle is 1,800 miles thick and appears to be layered, to consist of different materials at different depths. It accounts for about 85 per cent of the earth's volume, yet it is the most mysterious part of our planet. Scientists know that it is made of rock, but they do not know what kinds of rock. They know, too, that in some ways the mantle acts like a solid. In other ways it acts like a very gummy liquid. Many of the forces that cause the earth to seethe and stir appear to originate in the mantle.

Within the mantle lies the core. It consists of two layers, as a Danish scientist, Inge Lehmann, discovered in 1936. Studying what happened to earthquake waves deep within our planet, Miss Lehmann concluded that there must be a solid inner core surrounded by a molten, or liquid, outer core. Today scientists believe that the inner core has a diameter of about 1,580 miles, that it is probably made of dense metals such as iron and nickel, and that it is solid. The outer core, they believe, is 1,380 miles thick and molten.

The whole core, scientists reason, must be extremely hot, for it is under enormous pressure. Temperatures in the core may be as high as 8,000 degrees Fahrenheit.

The mantle and lower crust are also very hot. But here scientists have more direct proof.

The deeper men dig into the crust the higher the temperature rises. Some of South Africa's deep gold mines have had to be air-conditioned to keep workers from collapsing with heatstroke. Deep oil wells reach rock that is hotter than 212 degrees Fahrenheit (the boiling point of water at sea level). In most land areas the temperature goes up about one degree Fahrenheit for every 50 to 85 feet men dig down.

Volcanoes also offer proof of great heat inside the earth. Lava pouring out of the earth in an eruption may have a temperature of 2,000 degrees.

Scientists think that this heat is generated in the deep crust and in the mantle by radioactivity.

Several of the earth's elements—such as thorium, uranium, potassium, and radium—are radioactive. This means that they give off parts of themselves in the form of atomic particles. The particles in turn lose energy—which is heat.

The amount of heat caused by radioactivity is very small. But little of it escapes through the crust because rock is a poor conductor of heat. So the heat accumulates within the earth. Given enough time, the heat becomes very great.

Suppose, for example, radioactivity raised the interior temperature 1/1,000 of a degree a year. Over

Volcanoes offer proof of great heat inside the earth. Here molten lava erupts from Hawaii's Kilauea Iki.

just a million years the temperature would rise 1,000 degrees.

By slow accumulation, scientists think, heat in the mantle has become great enough to melt any kind of rock we know. Yet evidence shows that the rock acts like a solid, as well as a liquid.

The passage of certain earthquake waves indicates that the mantle is solid. So does the fact that some earthquake centers lie in the mantle. Where earthquakes occur the rock must be solid enough to break.

But studies of the earth's heat show that the mantle is hot enough to be molten. And other studies show that it acts like a very gummy liquid. For one thing, it can flow. For another, the earth's crust floats on the mantle and can move up and down in it. (Hawaii, for instance, moves up and down four inches every day under the moon's gravitational pull.)

These facts forced scientists to conclude that the mantle is both a solid and a liquid. That is, the mantle is a solid that also acts like a liquid. It is hot enough to be molten. But the tremendous pressure of the rocks above keeps the mantle solid.

Laboratory experiments showed that this might well be the case. In one experiment, ice was placed under 600,000 pounds of pressure and heated to 212 degrees. It did not melt but remained solid.

Deep within the earth, then, "solid" and "liquid" do not mean what they do to us on the surface. Under great pressure and in great heat, matter be-

haves in ways scientists are just beginning to understand. And so the portrait of the earth contains
many large question marks.

New question marks are constantly being added.
Scientists keep turning up new questions as they
seek the answers to old ones.

To take one example: Scientists set out to measure
the tiny amount of heat that does escape from the
inside of the earth through the crust. They had
always believed that heat flow would be greater
through the granite crust of the continents than
through the basalt crust of the oceans. The thick
granite is more radioactive than the basalt.

The measurements produced a surprise. Heat flow
is about the same in both kinds of crust. Why this
should be so, no one knows.

More measurements turned up another surprise.
In certain parts of the ocean floor the heat flow is
several times greater than normal.

Again, no one knows for sure why this is so. But
many scientists think the answer may be currents in
the mantle that carry heat from the core to the
crust. They compare what may happen with the
heating of water in a saucepan.

Water at the bottom of the pan heats first. The
heated particles expand, become lighter, and rise. As
these warm particles reach the surface, they move
around in swirls and currents. They give up some
heat to the cold water at the surface. Then they are
pushed aside by warmer water rising from the bot-

tom. Cooler and denser now, the particles sink.

These movements set up what is called a convection current. In a convection current, warmer material from the bottom keeps rising, while cooler material from the top sinks.

Many scientists think that the mantle contains huge convection currents, with diameters of 4,500 to 6,000 miles. Perhaps a convection current starts where the hotter core touches the cooler mantle. Or perhaps it is caused by greater radioactivity in the lower mantle. In either case, the greater heat could start a flow of hot rock toward the crust.

If such currents exist, they must move very slowly

In a pan of warming water, convection currents form as warmer particles rise and cooler particles are carried down. Many scientists believe that similar currents are at work in the earth's mantle.

because the mantle is extremely gummy. A slug of hot material might move upward at only four inches a year. At that rate it would require 30 million years to move from the bottom of the mantle to the bottom of the crust. But 30 million years is a short span in the 4 or 5 billion years of the earth.

Scientists would like very much to know whether or not convection currents move in the mysterious mantle. If they do, the currents would help explain the areas of high heat flow in the crust. And they might help answer one of the biggest questions in the portrait of our planet: Why does the earth have continents?

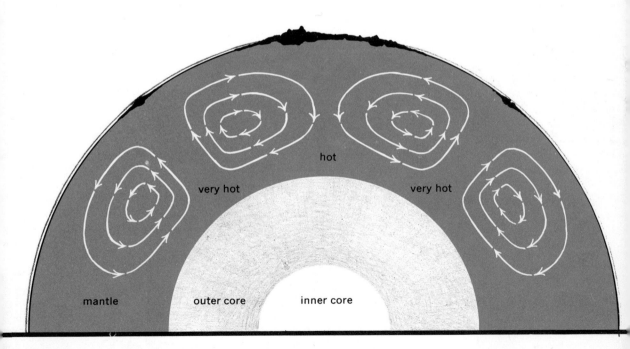

Why Continents?

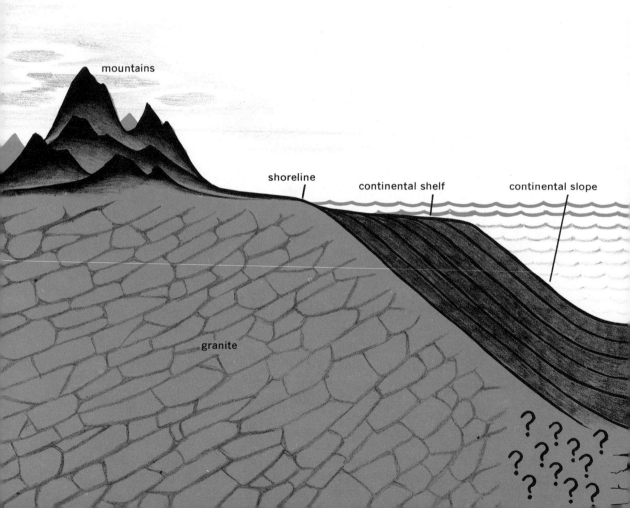

mountains

shoreline

continental shelf

continental slope

granite

"Why does the earth have land?" sounds like the kind of question a small child might ask. It is also the kind of question serious scientists ask. They would very much like to know why light rock should be bunched together on some parts of the earth's surface and not on others. Whatever the reason, they think this is a remarkable state of affairs. For continents are the exception, not the rule, on our planet. Nearly three quarters of the earth is covered with oceans, under which lies a crust of basalt.

In a few places, though, great chunks of granite rise above the oceans, forming continents. The continents are something like icebergs, since only their tops can be seen. Most of an iceberg's bulk lies beneath the ocean surface. Most of a continent's huge bulk reaches down into the mantle. In fact, scientists often speak of the continents as floating in the mantle.

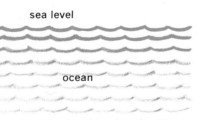

sea level

ocean

The continents do not end at the shoreline. Rather, shelves of continental rock reach out into the water, sloping gently down. Some distance out, the shelves end abruptly and plunge sharply down to the ocean floor. Here granite meets basalt, and this is the true dividing line. Exactly how and where granite meets basalt is not known, as the question marks indicate.

basalt

It is also true, of course, that the whole crust floats in the softer, denser mantle. And this fact offers a kind of answer to the question of why the earth has continents. The granite, being lighter rock, floats higher than the basalt.

But that is not the kind of answer that satisfies a scientist. It does not explain where the granite came from; why it is at the earth's surface; or why it is bunched together in places.

Over the years a number of theories have attempted to explain why the earth has continents. Today there are two theories that seem very promising.

One was developed by J. Tuzo Wilson of the University of Toronto.

Wilson thinks that about 3 billion years ago the earth was largely covered with oceans. But here and there small islands rose above the water, probably pushed up by pressure within the earth.

The islands bulked very small in the huge expanse of ocean, but they were the first land. And they were the cores from which our present continents grew. Wilson believes that several of these cores are recognizable today. One is the very old area of rock called the Canadian Shield. Another is the land mass we call Scandinavia. Still others lie in Africa and Australia.

The Canadian Shield was where Wilson began his studies. Near the Great Lakes he found two flat areas, each made of ancient lavas, with gold running

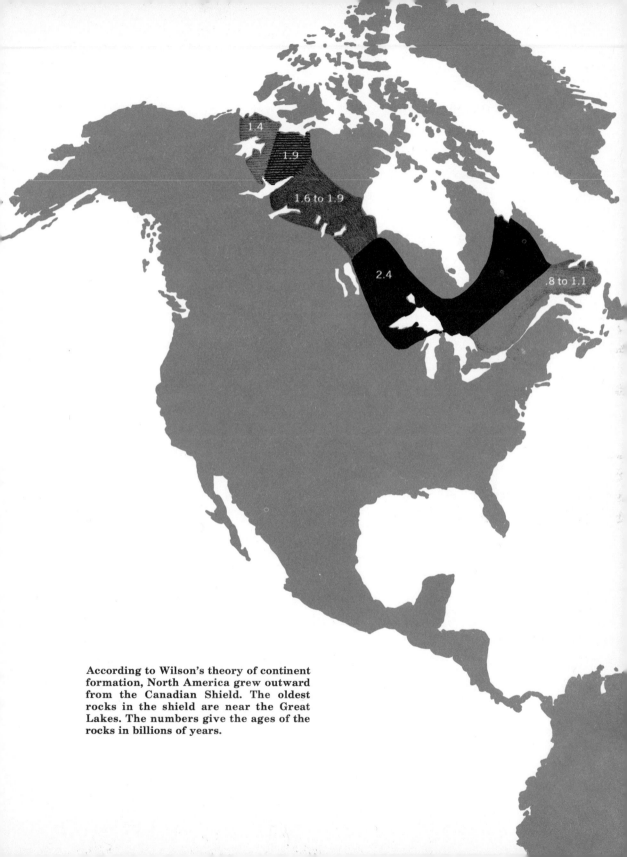

According to Wilson's theory of continent formation, North America grew outward from the Canadian Shield. The oldest rocks in the shield are near the Great Lakes. The numbers give the ages of the rocks in billions of years.

through them. A different kind of rock circled the two flat areas.

How old were the various rocks? Wilson found out through a scientific method called radioactive dating. The rocks contained radioactive elements. These elements give off parts of themselves at a fixed and known rate. So by measuring the amount of radioactivity left in them, it is possible to work backward and discover how long ago the rock formed. The gold-bearing lavas turned out to be about 2½ billion years old. The surrounding rocks were a good deal younger—1½ billion years old. The farther Wilson went from the core of the shield, the younger the rocks turned out to be, in laboratory tests. Along the Atlantic coast they were only half a billion years old.

The rock ages suggested that North America had grown outward from a central core. Later studies of the other cores showed a similar pattern. Rocks were oldest at the core and grew steadily younger in the outer areas.

These discoveries raised many questions. A major one was: How could continental cores have grown?

Wilson thought he knew the answer. As soon as the first cores formed, he pointed out, erosion must have started. Wind and rain chewed at the cores, breaking off tiny fragments. These grains of sand and rock washed down from the land to form beaches and broad underwater shelves.

For millions and millions of years, erosion wore down the cores, and sediments piled up thicker and

38

thicker. Eventually, the earth's crust sagged under the weight of the sediments. It fractured in long, arc-shaped cracks, setting off violent earthquakes. Along the great cracks undersea volcanoes formed. In eruption after eruption, they poured forth vast quantities of lava and built lofty cones. In time the cones rose above the surface of the ocean. They formed the curving strings of islands we call island arcs.

Between the islands and the land cores lay broad, shallow seas. Sediment continued to wash into these seas. Finally, by some unknown process, a huge uplift took place beneath the seas. The areas were lifted high above sea level and joined to the existing land.

In much this way, Wilson thinks, the continents grew and grew, gaining over the sea as their sediment washed into it. He thinks, too, that the same process must be going on today. Erosion continues. Sediment washes into the oceans. And new land must be forming.

If Wilson is right, there are several places where we can observe the slow process of continent-building. One is off the coast of Asia. Here the arc of volcanic islands has risen—Japan. Between Japan and the mainland lies the broad, shallow China Sea. It is slowly but steadily being filled in by sediments. Some are washed down from the mountainous islands of Japan. Some are poured in by the Hwang Ho and Yangtze rivers of China.

However, Wilson's theory is not accepted by all earth scientists. Many prefer a different theory. It

39

was first put forward by F. A. Vening-Meinesz, a Dutch expert on gravity and the earth's interior. Since then, it has been developed by others, among them Maurice Ewing of Columbia University's Lamont Geological Observatory.

According to this theory, continent-building began when the earth was very young. It was still so hot that no hard crust had formed on its surface. Many changes were taking place in the materials of the young earth. And deep inside, granitic materials formed. They were caught up in convection currents.

The currents of soft material rose from the center of the earth. They spread out on the surface, cooled, and then sank, replaced by hotter, rising material.

However, the light granite was not carried down in the convection currents. It was left behind on the surface like a kind of scum. As the currents continued to rise, they carried up more and more granite. As the currents spread out at the surface, they swirled the granite scum around.

Some scientists think that swirls of granite accumulated in several places. There, during a couple of billion years, the granite grew into giant patches. The granite patches were lighter than the rock around them. And so they floated higher in the mantle— becoming the continents.

Other scientists, among them Vening-Meinesz and Ewing, think that something different happened. They think that all the granite accumulated in one place, forming a huge super-continent.

40

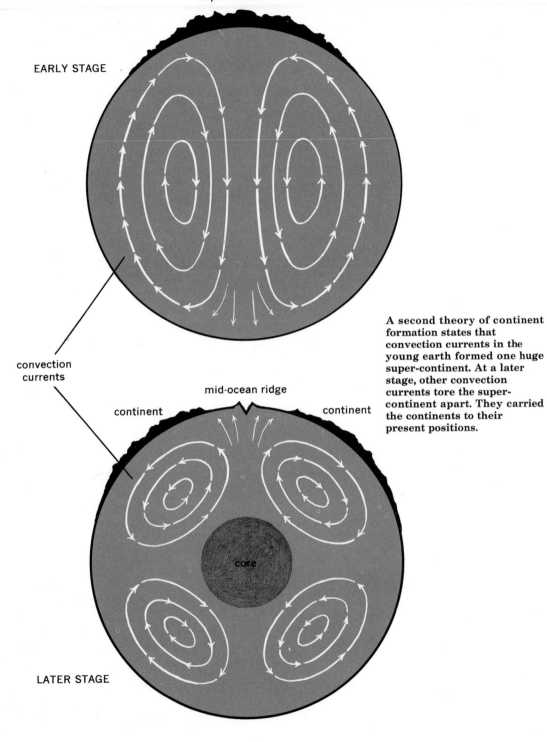

super-continent

EARLY STAGE

convection
currents

mid-ocean ridge

continent   continent

core

LATER STAGE

A second theory of continent formation states that convection currents in the young earth formed one huge super-continent. At a later stage, other convection currents tore the super-continent apart. They carried the continents to their present positions.

Convection currents continued to rise under this big land mass. As they spread out, they dragged at its bottom. In time the land mass cracked. And, very slowly, the crack grew. As it grew, one piece of the huge land mass was carried westward. Over millions of years, the crack grew into the Atlantic Ocean and the westward-moving land became the Americas.

Meanwhile, other cracks, caused by convection currents, had split off smaller pieces of the super-continent. These became Australia and Antarctica. Still other cracks swung pieces of the super-continent around, but did not tear them loose.

It is a strange picture these scientists paint—of swirls of granite becoming a super-continent, of the super-continent breaking into pieces, of smaller continents moving huge distances over the face of the earth. But in the earth's time scale, tiny yearly movements can add up to great changes.

The picture, of course, may or may not be true. Convection currents may or may not exist. And if they do exist, they may or may not have been the force that formed our continents.

Still, there is evidence that makes this theory a very tempting one.

For one thing, if the continents could be pushed about, they would fit together amazingly well. A glance at a map shows you how the Americas fit against Europe and Africa. The eastern bulge of Brazil fits into the Gulf of Guinea. The western bulge of

Africa, together with western Europe, fills the great hollow between Nova Scotia and Trinidad. Where the bottoms of South America and Africa then come together, Antarctica fits in. Australia goes beside Antarctica and India.

If the continents were once fitted together this way, then they should share certain geographic features. And they do. Striking similarities exist, for example, between the eastern regions of the Americas and the western regions of Europe and Africa.

Both have old, worn mountain ranges full of coal deposits.

Both have similar inland seas—the Mediterranean and the Caribbean. Each sea runs from east to west. Each lies between large land masses. Each is peppered with islands and peninsulas. Each is dotted with volcanoes. All this suggests that they might once have formed a single inland sea that was cut in two.

Then there is fossil evidence. A fossil is the remains of an animal or plant that lived in an ancient era. Fossils can be bones, shells, or footprints. They can also be impressions in rock of plants, animals, or insects.

Fossil evidence shows that the same plants and animals developed at the same time in areas that are now far apart. To take just one example, fossil remains of a small reptile called *Mesosaurus* have been found in only two places in the world: the east coast of South America and the west coast of Africa. It is

43

most unlikely that *Mesosaurus* developed at the same time in these two distant areas and only in these areas. It is much more likely that the reptile developed in just one place. Drifting continents is one way of explaining such fossil finds.

Another peculiar find has to do with a glacier that covered part of South America in an ancient ice age. Marks left by the glacier indicate that it must have climbed out of the sea onto South America's east coast. But this is impossible. Glaciers are land ice and cannot form in the sea. One possible explanation is that eastern South America once lay next to another land mass and has since drifted away.

The theory of drifting continents was first seriously suggested in 1915 by a German geologist named Alfred Wegener. Wegener argued that since continents could move up and down in the mantle, they could also move sideways. He believed that the granite continents had plowed through the ocean floor of basalt. Basalt, he said, was so weak that it could not resist any pressure.

Actually, as scientists later discovered, basalt is far

These three maps show how our present-day continents might have "drifted" apart from one great super-continent.

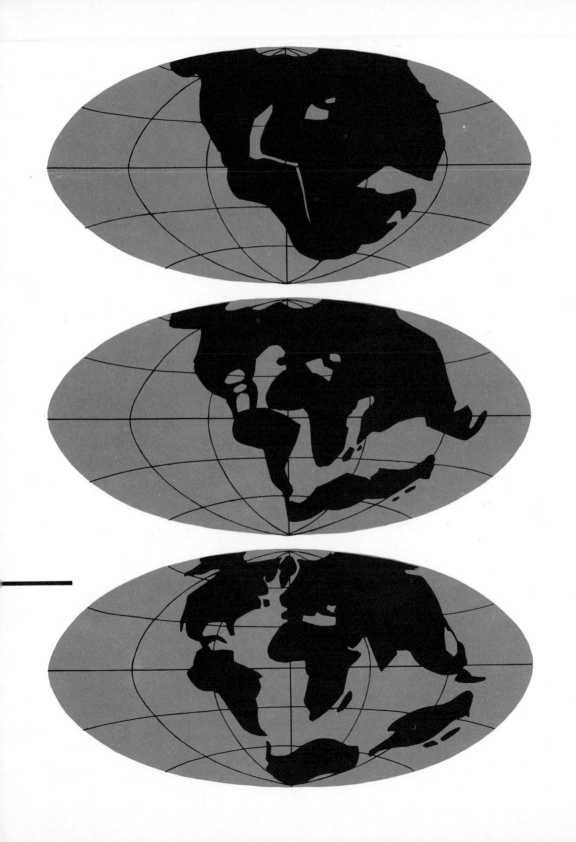

from weak. It is much denser than granite, and the continents could not possibly plow through it. With this discovery, Wegener's theory no longer stood up. But the evidence pointing to continental drift continued to fascinate people. And today the theory of convection currents has given new life to the theory of continental drift.

Many scientists, however, do not believe in continental drift. They do not believe that the Americas have drifted some 3,000 miles from Europe and Africa. Nor do they believe that the Atlantic Ocean was born as a crack in a super-continent. But they, like believers in drift, are interested in testing the theory.

If the Americas have drifted westward, there is every reason to think that they are still drifting. This can be tested by measuring the distance between the Americas and Europe-Africa.

Until recently, there was no way to make a precise measurement. The distance was known only in miles, not in yards or feet. But now earth scientists have a new instrument called the Danjon Impersonal Astrolabe, which enables them to use the stars in measuring the positions of points on the earth. With it they can estimate the distance between any two points to within five or ten feet.

This method, of course, requires a good deal of time. If the continents move, they do so very slowly —traveling perhaps an inch a year. So scientists would have to wait another 50 or 100 years before they could take a meaningful second set of measurements.

Investigation of other secrets of the earth may also shed light on the theory of drift.

During the IGY, oceanographers explored several great rifts in the sea bottoms. At present the rifts cannot be explained. But further study may show whether they are part of a splitting process. If they are, this will strengthen the case of believers in drift.

Studies of mountains also come into the picture. Mountain-building is the result of mighty, unseen forces and may be related to drift.

For example, believers in drift think that India has separated from South Africa during the past 70 million years. They suggest that when India slid into Asia part of the earth's crust buckled and forced up the Himalaya Mountains.

Drift could explain conditions along the Pacific coast of the Americas. This is a region of active volcanoes and earthquakes. Here, too, young high mountains rise abruptly out of the sea. These facts suggest movement—movement that crumples the crust and forces up mountain ranges.

Then again, continental drift is simply theory. And there are many other explanations of how the earth's mountains are built.

Tall
Mountains
and
Deep
Holes

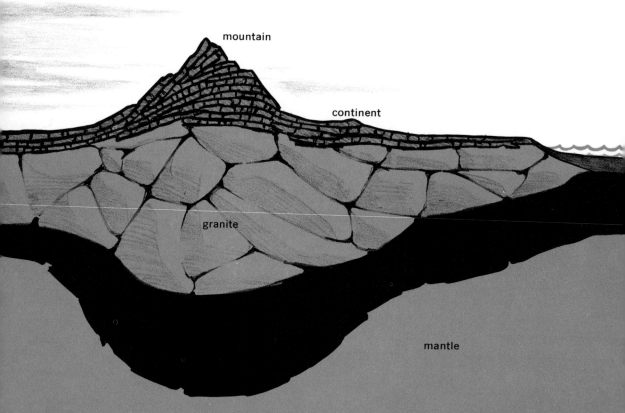

mountain

continent

granite

mantle

Some 200 million years ago the earth was stirring. Vast sections of its crust heaved and twisted, bending, folding, and upending layers of rock. And where this happened, great new chains of mountains rose. One such chain reached from Newfoundland to Alabama, its towering, snow-capped peaks jagged against the sky. In the time that followed, wind, rain, and frost attacked the lofty peaks. Fragment by fragment, grain by grain, they were worn down. Today they are the low and gentle, rounded mountains we call the Appalachians. In some future age they will vanish, worn down to their very roots.

The world's mighty mountains seem to us unchanging and unchanged, for a man's lifetime is not even a second in the life of these mountains. Yet they are forever changing. They are thrust out of the crust in great upheavals. They are sculptured and worn down by wind and rain and frost.

For reasons scientists do not understand, the earth

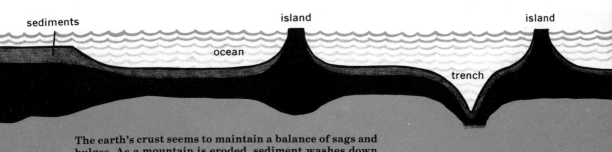

sediments · island · ocean · trench · island

The earth's crust seems to maintain a balance of sags and bulges. As a mountain is eroded, sediment washes down on the lowlands. Added weight here causes deep-lying plastic material to flow toward an area of less pressure —under the mountain, which has grown lighter because of erosion. As the plastic material flows under the mountain's roots, it lifts the mountain higher.

The earth's mountains are ever changing. This lofty, sharp peak in the Andes is part of a chain of young mountains that will one day be worn down into gentle, rolling hills like the Appalachians.

50

goes through periods of mountain-building. These times are called revolutions, and in the earth's history there have been at least ten of them. The Appalachian Revolution began between 200 and 300 million years ago. We live now in what is called the Cascadian Revolution. It began about 60 million years ago, long, long before man appeared on the earth. Among the mountains it has produced are the Alps, the Rockies, the Andes, and the Himalayas. These are all folded mountains that have buckled out of the crust. They are the world's mightiest chains of mountains. And they are the mountains scientists least understand.

Earth scientists have seen volcanoes grow. They have watched as erosion etched high plateaus into mountains. But the folded mountains—these are the giants that the human eye cannot catch in action. These are the giants whose secrets men have sought for years.

About 200 years ago scientists first probed the world's big mountains to find out what they were made of. The answer was a surprising one. The mightiest of mountains were made of sediment. It was sediment that had been washed from the land into ancient, vanished seas. There, as ages passed, it was packed down into rock, stirred and changed under tremendous pressure and heat, and then somehow thrust miles into the sky. The proof lay in the rocks themselves and in the fossils of sea life found two or three miles up great mountains in the Alps, the

Rocky Mountains, and the Himalayas.

What force could have thrust up massive mountain systems from the bottom of the seas? What force could have bent, crumpled, tilted, and broken the layers of rocks in the folded mountains? No one knew, and no one knows today, though there are many theories about mountain-building.

For a long time scientists believed that a cooling of the earth might explain the folded mountains. They thought that the earth was born hot and had been cooling ever since. If the earth were cooling, the regions under the solid crust would shrink. This would cause the crust to wrinkle, fold, and buckle, just as the skin of a withering apple is forced into ridges and folds as the pulp inside shrinks.

Today's scientists no longer believe that possible. They say the earth could not have shrunk enough to account for all the ranges of folded mountains. Also, many scientists doubt that the earth is cooling. They think it may be warming up because of internal radioactivity.

So earth scientists have turned to other theories of mountain-building.

One important theory was advanced in 1889 by the American geologist Clarence Dutton, who had made a wide study of our western mountains. Dutton concluded that the earth maintains a balance of sags and bulges. To describe this balance, he coined the word *isostasy;* it comes from Greek roots meaning "equal standing" or "equal pressure."

Layers of sediments from ancient seas were raised and folded, forming these mountains in Montana.

Broadly speaking, Dutton explained, the earth's sags were the ocean basins, made of heavy, dense material. The bulges were continents and islands, made of light material. But the sags and bulges were also an important part of mountain-building.

As mountains are eroded, Dutton said, huge amounts of sediment are washed onto low-lying areas. As the sediment accumulates, its weight grows greater and greater. In time, the sediment causes the earth's crust to sag. Sagging forces the underlying, softer material to flow. It flows to an area of less pressure —under the mountain, which is growing lighter and lighter because of erosion. As the softer material flows into the area of less pressure, it forces the mountain up.

Dutton used this theory to explain many mountain ranges of the American West that stand on broad, lofty platforms. All of these mountains had been greatly eroded, but still stood high. Dutton calculated that the weight of sediment washed from the mountains was great enough to force up the platform. This kept the mountains high.

Dutton's theory also called for the thrusting up of mountains along shorelines—which was exactly where many major mountain ranges were found. Here, he said, sediment washed from the land had caused the ocean crust to sag. As a result, long, narrow belts of mountains were forced up in the lightened continents.

Such mountain-building requires two conditions. One is a great weight of sediment. The other is a weak area in the crust. Given these, mountains are raised as the earth maintains a balance between highlands and lowlands.

Modern scientists think there is much to be said for Dutton's theory. But they believe it could account for only some of the world's great mountains. Other explanations are also needed.

A second major theory has to do with the accumulation of sediment in ancient seas.

In ages past, huge but shallow inland seas covered areas that are now land. Such a sea once reached over most of Canada and the United States, stretching from Newfoundland to the Gulf of Mexico. And there are traces of seas in the hearts of other continents.

In these seas great troughs, or trenches, formed. They were caused by unknown forces.

Over hundreds of millions of years, rivers and streams washed sediment into these ancient seas. The sediment began to accumulate in certain troughs, along with the remains of millions of sea creatures. Age after age the unknown forces deepened the troughs. Age after age sediment continued to accumulate.

As the troughs pressed deeper into the earth, the lower layers of sediment were carried down to depths of perhaps 10 to 20 miles. There they became very hot. They were so soft that pressures stirred them and caused them to flow. For millions of years the sediment and remains of sea creatures were subjected

55

to great heat and pressure.

Then a change took place. The unknown forces relaxed. The sediment-filled trough was no longer drawn down into the earth. Rather, the crust at the trough began to rise. And so sediment rose from beneath the sea to become mountains like the Alps and the Rockies. With it the sediment bore fossils that tell of time spent beneath the sea.

Isostasy and sediment-filled troughs may account for many of the earth's big chains of mountains. But it is possible that still other causes are involved. Changes in the earth's heat and chemical make-up may affect mountain-building. Continental drift—if it occurs—may be a cause. And so may convection currents.

According to one theory, mountains are built when two convection currents flow toward each other. The two currents rise thousands of miles apart, spread out, and flow toward each other under the crust. As they flow, they drag at the crust, pulling it along.

When the two currents meet, they sink. But the crust remains at the surface. Under tremendous pressure from the sinking currents, it buckles into long wrinkles, or mountains.

The chief weakness in this theory, of course, is that no one knows whether convection currents exist. Can deep rock that is solid enough to break and cause earthquakes flow like plastic? At present scientists can only guess. And this guess plays a very important part in all theories about mountain-building and continent-building. If scientists knew more about these deep rocks, they would be much closer to learning some of the earth's big secrets.

And that is the reason behind Project Mohole: a plan to drill a hole through the crust and Moho into the mantle.

Project Mohole was suggested a few years ago by a group of United States scientists. It called for drilling the big hole in a place where crust and mantle are typical of a large part of the earth's area. It called for drilling in a place where the mantle was as accessible as possible.

To meet these conditions scientists decided to drill their hole in the bottom of an ocean. Oceans cover nearly three quarters of the earth's surface. So the crust beneath the oceans is more typical than continental crust. Also this crust, though dense and hard to drill into, is much thinner than continental crust.

Even so, Project Mohole was not going to be easy. It demanded a drilling rig stationed, somehow, in water 18,000 feet deep. It demanded a hole drilled through 15,000 feet of crustal rock. In all history, no one had even attempted to drill such a hole. To do so would require development of a new drilling technique, several million dollars, and years of time.

Nonetheless, a decision was made to go ahead with the first of a series of Moholes. For corings from the big holes will provide priceless evidence on how the earth was formed and what it is made of. Most important, this will be direct evidence—the kind of evi-

57

Drilling ship (above) carrying miles of drill pipe (next page) for Project Mohole. Soviet scientists are also attempting to drill through the earth's crust. However, they are drilling on land. They will try to reach the Moho by drilling on the Kurile Islands, where they believe the crustal rock is relatively thin.

dence earth scientists most need.

From a Mohole, scientists will learn much about the earth's heat and its radioactivity. For the first time they will have samples of the deep crust and upper mantle. They will learn what the deep rocks

are made of. They can then test such rocks in laboratory experiments to learn what they are like under conditions of great heat and pressure.

A series of Moholes will not solve all the mysteries of our planet. But scientists will finally be able to test theory against fact. They will better be able to interpret the land features they have long studied. And they will come closer to understanding the recently charted features of the earth's unseen face.

An
Unseen
Face

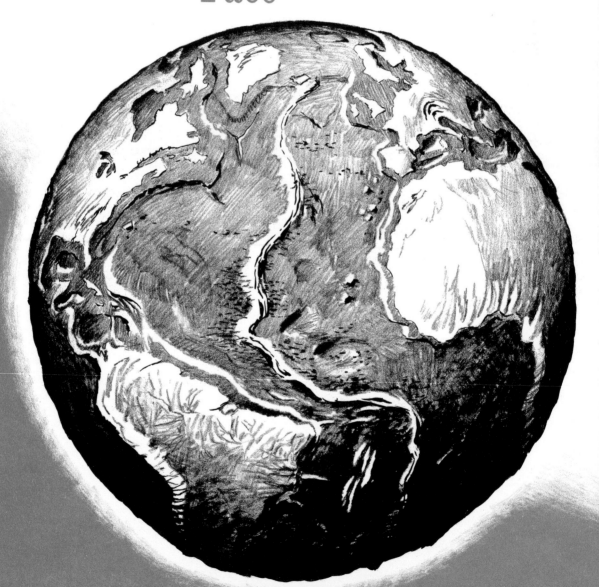

Oceans cover 71 per cent of the earth. Yet until a few years ago, scientists knew more about the face of the moon than they did about the ocean floors.

The reason was that they could see the moon. For more than 300 years scientists had been able to study the moon through telescopes. Only recently have they been able to probe the ocean depths with echo sounders, deep-sea cameras, and other modern instruments.

Exploration of the earth's unknown face reached its height during the IGY. And it shows that the earth's most rugged features lie beneath the oceans. Here are the tallest mountains and the deepest depths. Here, too, is a gigantic mountain range that circles the earth.

The beginning of this range is called the Mid-Atlantic Ridge and has been known for a number of years. IGY studies showed its extent. The ridge starts in the Arctic, runs south through the Atlantic, nears Antarctica, and then swings eastward around South Africa. There it joins the East Pacific Rise. The rise runs through the Indian Ocean, loops around Australia, continues across the Pacific, and reaches up the west coast of the Americas. Together, the Mid-Atlantic Ridge, the Indian Ocean Ridge, and the East Pacific Rise make up an earth-circling submarine range, 40,000 miles long.

The Mid-Atlantic Ridge is a tremendous swell in

If all the water were drained from the Atlantic Ocean, you would see the great mountain range called the Mid-Atlantic Ridge. Some of its peaks now rise above the ocean surface. They form islands, such as Iceland.

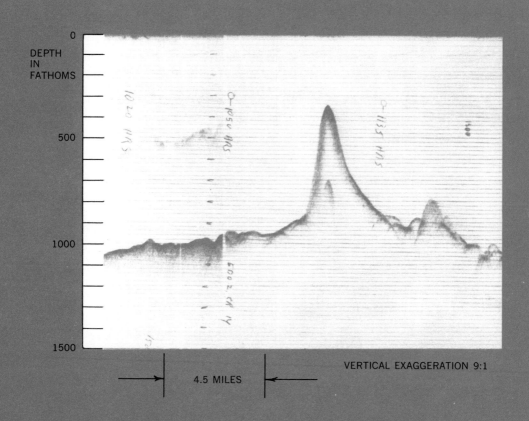

DEPTH
IN
FATHOMS

0

500

1000

1500

4.5 MILES

VERTICAL EXAGGERATION 9:1

Profile of a seamount, made by an echo sounder aboard a research vessel in the Caribbean Sea. The profile exaggerates the height of the seamount.

the earth's crust, 300 to 1,200 miles wide. The main feature of the Atlantic, it takes up a third of the ocean floor. Its highest peaks poke through the sur-

62

face, forming islands such as Iceland and the Azores. The ridge is volcanic and peppered with glowing cones.

The crest of the ridge is slashed here and there by a big rift that is 30 miles wide in places. In the South Atlantic the rift broadens into a trench that is 25,748 feet deep. (The other big Atlantic ditch is the Puerto Rico Trench. It is 27,510 feet deep—more than five miles. But it is not related to the mid-ocean rift.)

At the ridge's base are low, lumpy hills that level off into flat plains. The plains are the continents' dumping ground. Here currents drop huge amounts of sediment washed from the land. The sediment spreads out on the plains, which reach for miles on end across the Atlantic floor.

The flatness of the plains is broken only by seamounts and guyots. Seamounts are underwater mountains, some of which reach heights of three miles. Guyots are strange, flat-topped mounts.

The bowl-shaped Pacific is much more rugged than the Atlantic. It has almost no plains. Instead, the floor is rough with hundreds of seamounts and guyots, scores of mountain ranges and island chains, and a number of deep trenches. The Mariana Trench goes down nearly seven miles into the earth. The Tonga-Kermadec Trench is long enough to stretch from Kansas City to New York; it is so deep that it could swallow seven Grand Canyons. At the other extreme, Hawaii towers up six miles high from the

Pacific floor, which makes it the world's tallest mountain. Four great east-west cracks split the earth's crust under the Pacific. Up to 30 miles wide, the cracks are 10,500 feet deep and 3,300 miles long. They reach across 5 per cent of the earth's surface.

Scientists explore the ocean floor to answer the question, "What is it like?" But, as is often true in science, the answer to one question immediately raises new questions.

The guyots, for example, present a small but interesting puzzle. These mounts are probably lava spouts. But why are their tops flat? And, since the tops lie half a mile below the ocean surface, how does it happen that shallow-water fossils are embedded in them?

The flat plains present a much bigger problem. We know that they are built chiefly of sediment carried

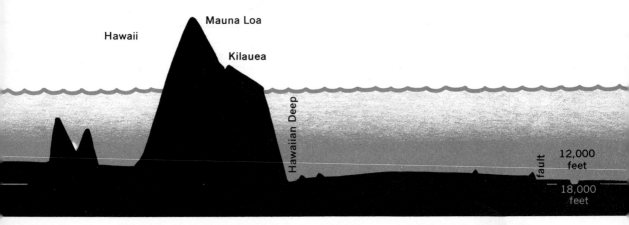

Hawaii is actually a volcano that rises 28,000 feet from the bottom of the Pacific and was built to that great height by countless flows of lava. (The drawing exaggerates the height.)

out from the land. Together with the remains of small sea creatures, the sediment has settled to the bottom, forming a plain as smooth as glass. The problem is that some of the sediment appears to be missing.

Scientists know the rate at which sediment is now being deposited. They are fairly sure about the number of years sediment has been laid down. Multiplying the two figures, they calculated that the sediment should be about three miles thick. Probing showed that it was only a third of a mile thick.

Beneath the soft sediment is a layer of something 1¼ miles thick. No one knows yet what this is, but some scientists hope it will turn out to be packed-down sediment. Otherwise they will face a big question: What has become of the missing 90 per cent of the sediment?

The plains fan out from the ends of yawning submarine canyons. And the canyons also raised a question: How had they formed?

This question, however, was answered. Maurice Ewing and an associate, Bruce C. Heezen, proved that the canyons were formed by turbidity currents.

Turbidity currents are submarine avalanches of mud. They are born on steep, downward slopes where great quantities of sediment have been deposited over hundreds of years. Sometimes the sediment breaks loose, stirred into motion by a violent storm or an earthquake. It tumbles down the continental slope, gathering speed as it goes and mixing with water to form a dense, liquid mud. This moving mass of liquid mud is a turbidity current. Moving at speeds of 50 miles an hour or more, it sweeps through the ocean, tearing apart everything in its path.

Ewing and Heezen showed that the submarine canyons were carved by these currents of mud, which then slowed and dropped their sediment on the plains.

So far, however, no one has been able to show how the ocean trenches formed. Like the rifts and ridges, they remain major scientific mysteries.

The trenches alone raise many questions. What are they? How did they form? Why are most of them in the Pacific? And why do these great gashes lie chiefly along the western rim of the Pacific?

IGY probes showed that the trenches are strangely alike. Their sides are steep. Their bottoms tend to be flat, perhaps because of landslides or of sediment that has settled in them. And the deeper trenches are all about 35,000 feet deep. These facts raise still more questions: Why are the trenches so deep? Why do the deepest ones stop at 35,000 feet? Does something in the earth's crust keep them from reaching deeper?

The Pacific trenches seem to be related to a number of other things. To name just three of these: The trenches lie in an area that is active with volcanoes and earthquakes. They lie parallel to island arcs. And they lie seaward of the mountain ranges that edge the western coast of the Americas. Some IGY scientists thought that trenches and earthquakes might be symptoms of mountain-building. But no one is sure.

Nor can anyone explain the rifts in the ocean

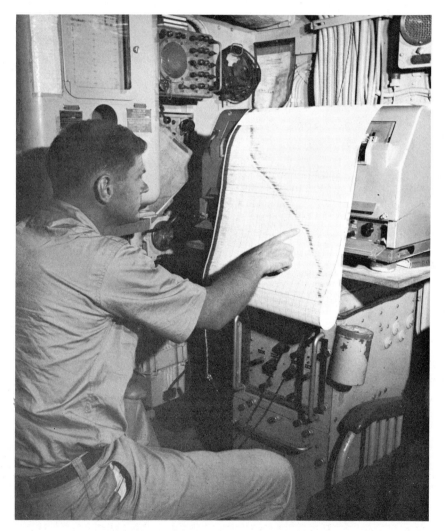

An oceanographer studies the profile of a deep Pacific trench.

floors. The rifts are clearly places where the earth has cracked open. But scientists do not know why it should crack.

Those who believe in continental drift are extremely interested in the great rifts of the Mid-Atlantic Ridge. They think that the ridge may mark the point where the Americas split away from Europe and Africa.

Others don't think so. But all agree that the ridge is a sign of great forces at work within the earth. The ridge has jagged peaks and deep rifts. It is volcanic. It is an earthquake center. And the flow of heat from it is greater than in surrounding areas.

Ewing thinks these facts support the idea of convection currents. He suggests that the ridge is a sign of up-flowing hot material that forces up mountains and heats the crust. The hot material may rise like a single fountain, or jet. Meeting the crust, it divides into two flows moving in opposite directions. The opposing pulls, Ewing suggests, cause the crust to crack.

The idea of convection currents was also supported by certain heat-flow measurements in the Pacific.

IGY ships measured the heat flow from Easter Island Rise, a north-south welt in the Pacific floor. In some places the flow was five times normal. A rising convection current would explain the high heat flow.

IGY ships also measured heat flow at the bottom of a trench that runs down the west coast of South America. Here the heat was very low—about 1/30 of what it had been on Easter Island Rise. This suggested a downward creep of cooling material under the earth's crust.

One of the IGY scientists who made these measurements was Roger Revelle of Scripps Institution of Oceanography in California. Revelle thinks that Easter Island Rise is a growing ridge that may one day become land. It grows as rock very slowly wells up. He thinks that rock is moving slowly downward under the trench. The slow downward movement sucks the bottom of the trench into the earth.

However, these are just first findings. They may be part of a broad pattern, but it is too early to tell for sure. Many other measurements of heat flow are needed.

Mohole drillings will help in these heat studies. They will also show whether crust near a ridge is newly formed, as it would be if the ridge was growing.

In fact, the Mohole's drill will open a fabulous history book that lies at the bottom of the oceans. Here the history of the earth is written in the rocks that formed age after age, in the sediments that have been laid down over millions of years.

The Mohole's drill will pass backward through time. It will pass through the age when the first air and water caused erosion. It will pass through the first crust that formed on our planet. Corings from the Mohole will tell us something about the earth's greatest secret: the way it was born and the way it grew into the planet of life.

Birth
of a
Planet

Scientists who seek the earth's greatest secret must reach back through the mists of time, for radioactive dating of rocks shows that the earth's birth took place between four and five billion years ago. The task seems impossible. Yet scientists have found a surprising number of clues about what happened.

They start with the fact that the earth is part of a family. The family is our solar system—the sun and the nine planets that orbit it. The planets are clearly related to one another and to the sun in a number

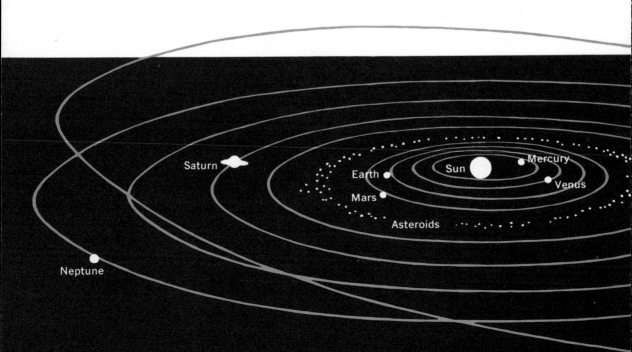

of ways. For example:

The sun and its planets form a unit in space.

If you could back off to the north and look at the solar system, you would see that all its major bodies move in a counter-clockwise direction. The sun and planets rotate counter-clockwise on their axes. The planets revolve counter-clockwise around the sun.

The orbits of the planets lie on nearly the same plane. (The one exception is Pluto's; but there is some question as to whether Pluto is really a planet.)

The planets are separated in an orderly way, by ever increasing distances.

The planets fall into two main classes. The inner planets are all small, solid bodies. The outer planets are giants wrapped in thick atmospheres.

Any theory about the birth of the planets must account for this broad pattern. And so all major

If you could watch our solar system from the north, you would see the earth and the eight other planets moving in an orderly arrangement, counter-clockwise around the sun.

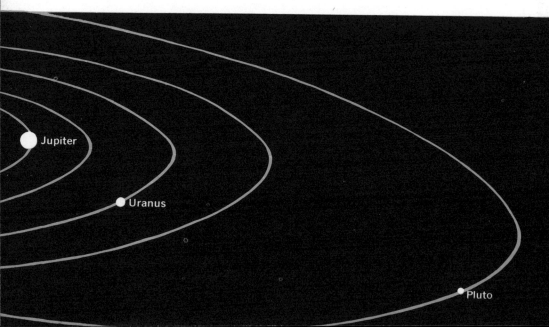

Jupiter

Uranus

Pluto

theories stem from one of two ideas:

(1) The planets formed from material torn out of the sun. Perhaps another star collided with the sun, splashing billions of tons of matter into space. Or perhaps another star passed so close to the sun that gravitational attraction drew matter out of the sun into space.

(2) The planets and the sun were born of a great cloud of dust and gas.

Most scientists today believe in the dust-cloud theory.

They suppose that about five billion years ago a vast cloud of dust and gas was floating in space. The tiny particles that composed the cloud were spread very thin, and the cloud probably measured trillions of miles in diameter.

The particles were moving a little. They tended to attract one another. And they were also being pushed together by the pressure of starlight. Drifting slowly over huge distances, the particles swirled in toward the center of the cloud. The cloud shrank in size.

Being smaller, the cloud was more dense. Since its particles were closer together, the forces of gravity among them increased. They moved faster and faster and became hotter and hotter.

The cloud continued to condense and contract. As it did so, it began to spin, slowly at first, then faster and faster. In time the cloud was spinning like the funnel of a gigantic whirlpool.

Eventually a huge part of the cloud collapsed in-

This photograph shows vast clouds of dust and gas in another part of our galaxy. In one small part of such a cloud, many scientists believe, our solar system may have formed.

ward, forming a great ball of gas. Still contracting and condensing, the ball was under such great pressure that it began to glow, sending out light and heat. When it did, a new star was born, the star we call our sun.

Meanwhile, the outer parts of the cloud had flattened into a spinning disk of dust and gas that whirled around the center. Whirlpools formed within the disk. In each whirlpool the dust particles, which were heavier, settled toward the center. There they began to collide. When two particles of the same size collided, they evaporated in the heat caused by the collision. When two particles of different sizes collided, the smaller was added to the mass of the larger. This process went on for hundreds of millions of years. Larger masses kept sweeping up smaller ones. The masses grew and grew—into the planets.

Each planet had a solid body and was wrapped in a thick envelope of gases. Radiation from the sun began to act on the gases, blowing away the lighter ones. Planets near the sun lost much of their atmosphere. Radiation from the sun had less effect on the more distant planets. They are still wrapped in thick atmospheres today.

That is the way most scientists believe our solar system came into being about 4.5 billion years ago. The sun was born of a cloud of dust and gas. The planets formed in the disk of leftover matter that circled the sun.

The newborn earth must have been very hot, and it grew even hotter. As it kept sweeping up matter, the collisions added heat to it. As matter packed itself around the central core, pressure grew so great

that heat was generated.

Heat and pressure caused many chemical reactions to take place inside the earth. Chemical compounds were built up and broken down. Heat continued to accumulate and eventually the young earth became molten. Then, scientists think, the core formed. Molten iron, being heavy and dense, flowed toward the center of the earth—perhaps at a rate of 50 thousand tons a second for 500 million years. The flowing iron displaced other, lighter materials, which rose toward the surface. There, as the young earth later began to cool, the lighter material hardened into a solid crust.

Underneath this first crust, the earth was still very hot. It spewed forth molten rock and released great clouds of steam and gas. Gravity kept the steam and gas from escaping into space. And so a thin atmosphere formed.

The sky above the young earth was black, for at first there was not enough atmosphere to scatter the sun's rays and make a blue sky. The thin atmosphere also resulted in extreme temperatures. By day the sun's unfiltered rays blazed on the surface of naked rock. By night the heat escaped through the atmosphere and water froze. As water in the rocks froze and thawed, grains of rock were broken off. The first erosion had occurred.

Sometime in this early stage the first rains fell. Water collected in tiny streams and ran down barren, rocky slopes. Tiny streams joined to form bigger

75

The planets probably formed in the disk of leftover matter circling the sun.

streams that raced down to low-lying plains. The water collected in puddles. Puddles grew into lakes. Then, as the lakes grew and grew, a sea formed, salty with chemicals from the earth.

The sun's heat drew water from the sea into the atmosphere. The water vapor condensed in the air and fell as rain. The rain collected in streams, which ran down to the sea. The streams carried and deposited tiny grains of sand, eroded from rock. Sediment was now being laid on the rocky crust.

New volcanoes erupted, releasing great quantities of water and gas. The water was added to the sea, which grew deeper. The gases were added to the atmosphere, which grew more dense.

By the time it was two or three billion years old, the earth had a cool, solid crust. Most of the crust was probably covered by a deep ocean. Land areas were rock, with a little sediment of rock fragments. The oceans, the rocks, the rivers were all barren and lifeless. But the stage was now set for life.

Scientists do not know—and may never know—exactly how life began. But they think that heat and lightning acted on certain gases in the atmosphere, forming amino acids, the building blocks of living matter. Raindrops carried the amino acids into the sea. There, by ways and means unknown, a piece of living protein was produced. It split in two, and the two also divided. The dividing continued. The great chain of life had been established.

Much later the first plants evolved. And they began to change the atmosphere. Like modern plants, they took carbon dioxide out of the air and released oxygen. Over many, many years, the amount of free oxygen in the air increased greatly. And oxygen is chemically very active. It attacked and changed other gases in the air. In time the atmosphere became what it is today—a mixture of nitrogen and oxygen, with just a trace of carbon dioxide and other gases.

With this atmosphere, the first animal life began. From it, over a very long time, higher forms of life developed. The earth became the small but remarkable planet we know today—the only one in our solar system that is known to support intelligent life.

The earth is just right for life in several ways.

It is the right distance from the sun. If it were as close as Mercury it would be too hot. If it were as far away as Saturn it would be too cold.

Then there is the way the earth rotates on its axis. Every part of our planet receives some sunlight. As seasons change or day becomes night, different parts of the earth get a chance to cool off or warm up.

The earth's mass is also just right for a planet of life. Mass determines the strength of gravity. And the earth's gravity is strong enough to hold captive both the atmosphere and the oceans. If gravity were weak, the earth would be as airless, dry, and barren as the moon.

But the earth is a planet of life because air, water, and sun combine to make it so.

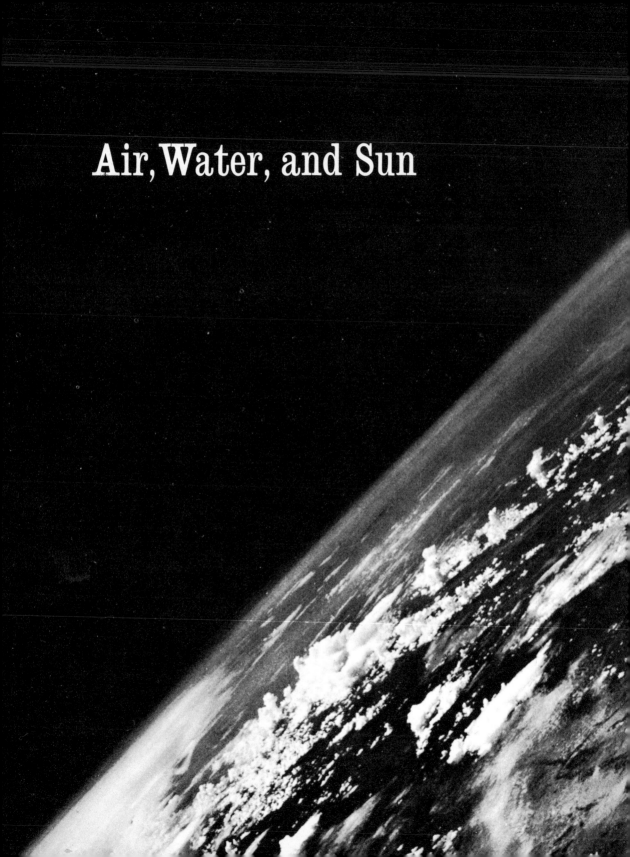

Air, Water, and Sun

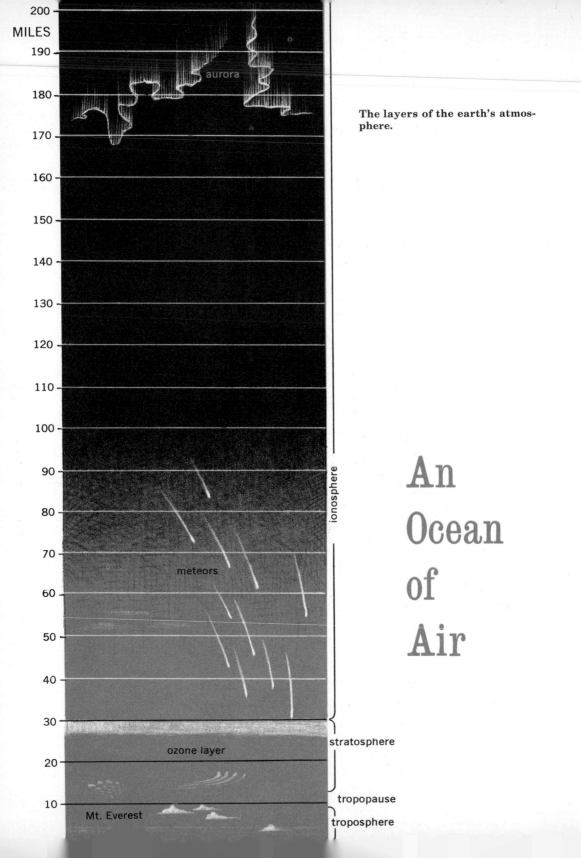

200
MILES
190
180 — aurora
170
160
150
140
130
120
110
100
90
80 — ionosphere
70
meteors
60
50
40
30
stratosphere
ozone layer
20
tropopause
10
Mt. Everest
troposphere

The layers of the earth's atmosphere.

An
Ocean
of
Air

As you read this, a column of air weighing about half a ton is resting on the top of your head. Similar columns rest on the heads of everybody else in the world.

That fact comes as a surprise to most people because we do not feel this great weight pressing on our heads. The reason is that our bodies are made to live under air pressure—and could not live without it. Just as some fish are made to live at the bottom of the seas, so men are made to live at the bottom of an ocean of air.

Because we are used to it, air often seems like nothing. We see through it and move through it with no trouble at all. Yet air is matter. It is made chiefly of gases.

About 78 per cent of the air is a gas called nitrogen. Most of the rest is oxygen, which men and animals depend on for life. The air also contains traces of other gases, such as carbon dioxide, ozone, argon, helium, and neon. In addition, the air carries salt crystals from oceans, dust from rocks, ash from erupting volcanoes, pollen from plants, dust from outer space, and still other kinds of matter.

Because it is matter, air has weight. At sea level, 14.7 pounds of air press constantly against every square inch of the earth's surface.

Air pressure is strongest near the earth's surface because this is the bottom of the atmosphere. Here the air molecules are packed together by the weight of air above. Higher up, the pressure is much less because the air is thinner. There its molecules are farther apart.

Rockets and satellites have found traces of the earth's thinning atmosphere thousands of miles above our planet. But most of the atmosphere is concentrated around the earth in a blanket several hundred miles thick. It is divided into layers, each different from the others.

The bottom layer, in which we live, is called the troposphere. Here most of our weather takes shape. The air carries the water vapor from which clouds and rain form. In it winds blow north and south, east and west. Air currents move up and down.

The troposphere is warmest near the earth's surface. This is because the sun heats the earth and the earth radiates heat that warms the air. As you go higher in the troposphere, temperatures drop steadily, then suddenly level off. The leveling-off point marks the beginning of the tropopause.

In the tropopause, winds reach their greatest force. This is the region of jet streams, winds that reach speeds of 300 miles an hour.

Above the tropopause is the stratosphere. In its lower parts, air is dry, clear, and cold. Most of the moisture, dust, and dirt have been left behind. Here, too, the air is much thinner. With fewer air particles to scatter the sun's light, the sky begins to darken. Blue changes to violet. Farther up the violet changes to black. The stars shine 24 hours a day and the sun blazes in the dark sky.

In the middle of the stratosphere, about 25 miles above the earth, the air begins to warm again. The cause of this warming is a layer of ozone, a gas that absorbs most of the sun's ultra-violet rays. One result is a belt of warm air in the stratosphere. A much more important result is that the ultra-violet rays cannot reach us in full force. These are the rays that cause sunburn. If all of them reached us, we would be fried alive.

In the upper layers of the stratosphere, the air cools again and violent winds blow. Near its top, the stratosphere begins to resemble the uppermost layer of the atmosphere: the ionosphere.

In the ionosphere the air is very thin, and it undergoes a great change. Here radiations from the sun break up atoms and molecules of gas into smaller particles that are electrically charged. Such particles are described as excited, or disturbed. Electric currents can flow through the ionosphere, just as they flow through the gas in a neon tube.

Beyond the ionosphere, thin traces of the atmosphere trail out perhaps 5,000 miles into space.

This vast ocean of air serves us in many ways. It provides the oxygen our bodies need. It shields us from the sun's ultra-violet rays. And it acts as a greenhouse roof, protecting the earth against extremes of heat and cold.

On the airless moon, the sun's rays blaze on the surface, heating rocks beyond the boiling point of water. Yet, after sunset, all this heat escapes into space. Temperatures drop from over 220 degrees to 300 below zero.

Because of the atmosphere, this does not happen on the earth.

The atmosphere cuts off a large amount of the sun's radiation. About 35 per cent is reflected back into space by clouds and dust in the atmosphere (and also by polar ice and snow). Another 18 per cent is absorbed by clouds, water vapor, and ozone. Only 47 per cent of the sun's radiation actually reaches the earth. This is enough to warm our planet but not to make it boiling hot.

The same heat continues to warm the earth after sunset because it is trapped by the atmosphere. The atmosphere acts like the glass in a greenhouse.

The glass allows the sun's heat and light to pass freely into the greenhouse. Plants and other materials absorb this radiation. But after a while they begin to give off heat in the form of invisible rays called infra-red. Infra-red rays cannot pass freely through the glass. Most of them are trapped in the greenhouse. That is why the greenhouse stays warm. Heat comes in and cannot escape.

Much the same thing happens with the earth's atmosphere. The 47 per cent of the sun's radiation passes freely through the atmosphere. The earth absorbs this sunlight, then gives off heat in the form of infra-red rays. The rays warm the air. But they cannot radiate freely away from the earth. Many of the infra-red rays are trapped by the

84

atmosphere. Moisture, ozone, and carbon dioxide block their path. The result is that the atmosphere tends to hold heat, rather than letting it escape into space.

So the earth is warmed by day, but not to the boiling point. It cools after sunset, but the temperature drops only a few degrees instead of some 500.

There is still another property of the atmosphere which helps sustain life on the earth. This is motion —the winds.

Winds distribute hot air from the tropics and cool air from the poles. They pick up moisture from the oceans and drop rain on the continents. They bring clean air into cities and sweep away the dirty air. Without winds the cities would be choked and the continents parched. The tropics would be unbearably hot and the rest of the world unbearably cold.

Fortunately, there is no chance that the atmosphere will ever fall into a dead calm all over the world. The earth has great wind systems that keep the air moving, day in and day out. The source of the energy that moves the winds is the sun.

The sun shines hottest on a wide belt of land and sea around the equator. This region absorbs more heat than any other part of the earth. And, as it gives off heat, it warms the air above it.

The hot air rises, cooling a little as it goes up. Then, pushed along by more hot air rising beneath it, the air flows away from the equator toward the poles, both north and south. There it is cooled, sinks to a lower altitude, and flows back toward the equator. Imagine, if you like, two big loops of moving air. One travels from the equator to the North Pole and back. The other travels to the South Pole and back.

In that way the winds are driven. Now a second

Great wind systems carry hot air away from the tropics and cold air away from the poles. (This is a simplified picture of systems that are complex and not yet completely understood.)

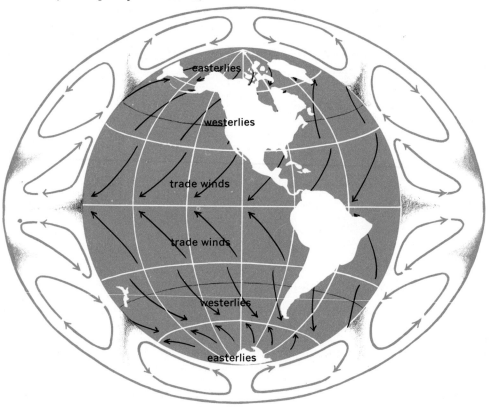

86

force enters the picture—the earth's rotation.

The earth rotates from west to east, carrying the atmosphere with it. This spinning puts a twist in the north-south flow of air. The twist produces the great westerly and easterly winds that sweep the world.

These winds would travel even faster than they do except for one thing—friction. The winds are slowed by contact with the ground. The contact also breaks the huge north-south loops into several smaller loops. And the smaller loops are, in turn, affected by the earth's uneven surface.

The sun's heat, the earth's spin, and friction— these are the three main things that account for the earth's winds. But scientists know that this picture is far from complete. They have not fully tracked the winds. They need to know much more about the jet streams and how these affect our winds and weather. They need to know more about exchanges of air between layers of the atmosphere.

It is clear that there are up and down movements of the atmosphere. Moist air from the troposphere is found in the stratosphere. Ozone from the strato-sphere is found in the troposphere. But how and why these exchanges take place, no one knows.

Such information is hard to come by because our ocean of air is vast. If it could be divided up for observation, every person in the world would have two million tons of air to watch.

Then, too, only the lowest part of the atmosphere

is fairly well known. Men have been studying surface winds for hundreds of years. They have been able to study upper layers of the atmosphere only since the coming of airplanes, high-altitude balloons, and rockets.

And, finally, winds cannot be studied alone, for they are only half of the big machine that distributes the sun's heat over the earth. They must be studied along with the other half of the machine: the oceans of water that cover nearly three quarters of the globe.

88

Facing page: Launching a
research rocket into the
upper air.

This page: A plastic balloon
used to explore the
atmosphere.

89

Oceans
of
Water

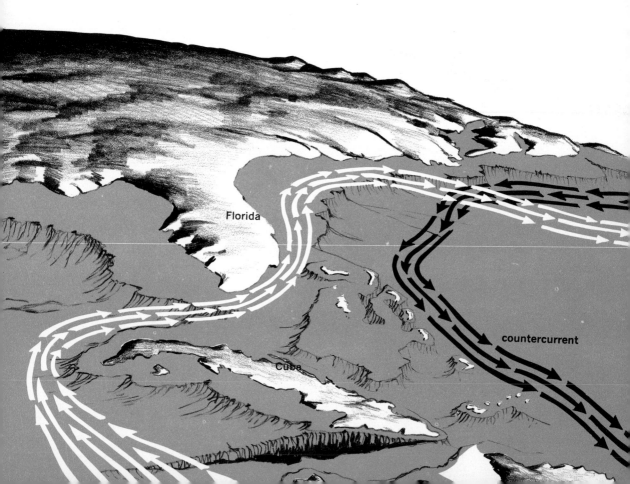

Florida

Cuba

countercurrent

Not long ago, the ocean temperature along the west coast of the Americas rose two degrees during a period of three years. This seemingly small change set off a chain reaction.

The warmer water drove away the tiny animals and plants called plankton.

Anchovies, small fish that feed on plankton, then moved away, following their food to colder waters.

Coastal birds that ate anchovies either starved or moved away.

And in Peru and Chile a major industry, which made fertilizer from bird droppings, was ruined.

Farther north, the warmer water either drove away or killed the cold-loving salmon. The California salmon industry was ruined. Canada's west-coast salmon fisheries were badly hurt.

To the south, long-established fishing grounds suddenly changed, as tropical fish followed warmer water

Gulf Stream

Bermuda

The Gulf Stream carries a vast amount of warm water from the tropics to the north. More than a mile below, a great countercurrent carries cold water from the Arctic to the south.

north. Albacore and marlin were caught off British Columbia, southern sea bass off Alaska, and sardines off California.

The same two-degree change in ocean temperature affected climate along the west coast of the Americas. The warmer ocean water released more heat into air. The warmer air produced a warmer climate.

No one really knows how or why this temperature change occurred in the Pacific. But its far-reaching effects make clear why earth scientists urgently need more information about the oceans. Changes in the oceans affect our food supply and the ways men earn a living. Changes affect climate, which influences men's activities in every part of the world.

Scientists studying the earth as a planet view the oceans as a major key to climate. The reason is that the oceans absorb, store, and release tremendous quantities of heat.

The oceans are the chief source of the heat that drives the winds. They supply this heat steadily because they gain and lose heat slowly—much more slowly than the land. The steady supply of heat keeps world temperatures fairly stable.

The oceans also distribute heat and cold to different parts of the earth. Ocean currents carry warm water away from the tropics. They carry cold water away from polar regions. Currents bring up cold water from the ocean depths. Warm surface currents heat the air and temper the climate in several parts of the world. For example, heat from the Gulf

Stream makes northwestern Europe a comfortable place to live. Without a warming current, this region would be as cold as Labrador and Baffin Island (which lie on the same degree of latitude).

Ocean currents, then, are the other half of the great machine that distributes the earth's heat and cold. Yet we know very little about them. Like the winds, they are extremely difficult to explore.

Oceans cover 71 per cent of the earth, are two to three miles deep, and contain 300 million cubic miles of water. That is a great deal of water to explore. Yet it must be explored from top to bottom if

Setting out one of a string of Nansen bottles.

93

scientists are to discover the movements of warm and cold water.

One way they do this is by lowering strings of Nansen bottles from a ship. The bottles, which have thermometers attached to them, trap water at different depths and measure the temperatures. When these measurements are made all along the ship's track, scientists gain a picture of temperature layers at various depths. This gives them many clues to the movements of cold and warm currents.

Chemical analysis of water from different depths also tells something about how the ocean waters circulate. For example, surface water takes in carbon-14 from the air, and it is carried along wherever the water goes. Carbon-14 is radioactive and can be dated. So scientists take samples of water at different depths and measure the amount of carbon-14 in it. This tells them how long ago the water was at the surface. It gives them clues to the circulation patterns of deep waters.

Through carbon-14 studies, IGY scientists discovered that deep, cold water wells up constantly in the Atlantic, replacing warm surface water. Its rate is such that the surface water is completely replaced once every 500 years. The result of this steady upwelling is that the air is cooler than it would otherwise be.

An even greater IGY discovery came about through the use of a new device: the Swallow float. Invented by John Swallow, a British scientist, it can be adjusted to float underwater at any depth scien-

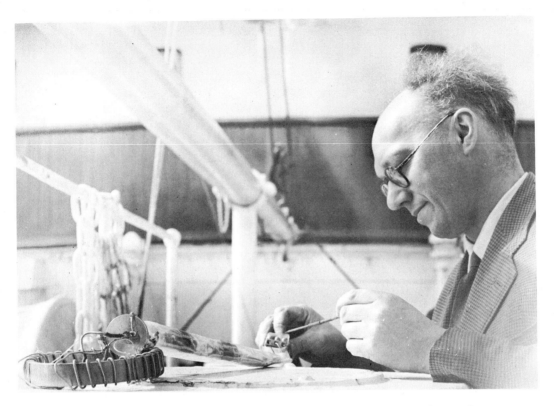

John Swallow aboard a research vessel, preparing a Swallow float for use far below the surface.

tists desire. The float sends out beeps by which it can be tracked. And so it is extremely useful for studying the movements of water below the surface. It was with the Swallow float that IGY scientists discovered some of the biggest ocean currents known to man. These currents are hidden from sight by thousands of feet of water.. They flow under surface currents, but in the opposite direction. For this reason they are called countercurrents.

Before this discovery, scientists had thought of

deep water as being fairly still. They knew that there was some movement in it. For instance, water at the bottom of the tropical Atlantic is so cold that it has clearly moved there from polar regions. But all the known currents lay at the surface, where they were apparently caused by the winds and the earth's rotation.

The only trouble was that there didn't seem to be enough currents. The Gulf Stream, for example, carries an enormous amount of water northward. It carries 17 cubic miles of water past a given point every second. Obviously some southward flowing current was replacing this water. But where was the current? Scientists could find no surface current big enough to balance the Gulf Stream.

A few scientists believed that there was only one possible solution to this puzzle. The Gulf Stream must be balanced by a powerful current that flowed unseen beneath the surface.

An American scientist, Henry Stommel, went a step further. He reasoned that the Gulf Stream must be replaced by water flowing south from the Arctic. Being colder and therefore denser, this water would flow deep below the surface as it headed south. In short, Stommel believed that the warm Gulf Stream had a cold countercurrent.

The Swallow float proved him right. Six thousand feet down in the Atlantic is a great, cold countercurrent. Seventy-five miles wide, it forms near the Arctic. There, for reasons scientists do not yet under-

96

stand, surface water sinks to the bottom. It flows south as a giant current, possibly rising to the surface in the Antarctic.

With this discovery, IGY scientists began a search for other countercurrents—and found several. One, the Pacific's Cromwell Current, had first been detected in 1951 but was not explored until 1958. The IGY showed it to be a giant among giants. Two hundred feet wide, it travels along the equator for 7,000 miles, carrying a thousand times more water than the Mississippi River.

How do these giant, unseen currents affect climate? How are they related to the winds? How do they form? What force drives them? How many countercurrents are there? These are just a few of the questions that the IGY discoveries have raised. And they have made the job of exploring the oceans bigger and more important than ever. For it is clear that scientists have barely begun to understand the ways in which the oceans affect our planet's climate.

Yet such understanding is vital. Oceans play a major part in forming today's climate. They carry seeds of change for the future. And they are, many scientists believe, the main clue to one of the earth's greatest mysteries: the ice ages.

The ice ages were the most sweeping climate change the earth has ever known. And until we understand them we cannot know whether we are living at the very end of the last ice age or whether that time of ice is far from finished.

Secrets
Locked
in
Ice

In the far, cold places of the earth great snows fell. They fell and they piled up, for the summer sun could not melt them all. The weight of new snows packed the old into ice. And then, as the weight kept growing, the ice began to flow. Creeping forward, great glaciers advanced from polar land and mountain tops.

The glaciers were mighty rivers of ice with wall-like tongues perhaps a mile high. Though they moved very slowly, nothing could stop them. Forests crumpled like matchsticks before them. Mountains and hills vanished under massive sheets of ice.

Blizzards swept the ice and added their snows to the glaciers. The ice grew thicker and flowed on, carving rock and gouging land. In time the ice covered a fourth of the earth's land. Huge areas of North America, Europe, and Asia lay under the glaciers' heavy hand. Winds blowing off the ice

During the Ice Age a vast, thick sheet of ice spread over much of the northern hemisphere (left), as glaciers flowed south from the Arctic (below).

turned nearby land into an almost lifeless tundra.

Finally, after thousands of years had passed, the ice began to melt. It drew back, releasing the land. As more time passed, the ice again stole forward, then melted. In the course of a million years, the glaciers advanced four times and retreated four times. They last retreated 10,000 years ago, leaving behind gigantic floods of melt-water as they drew back to the polar lands and the mountain tops.

There we see today the remains of the great glaciers of the Ice Age. And in now-green lands we see the marks of glaciers from that time of ice.

Since men first learned to read those marks, the Ice Age has been a major scientific mystery. What caused it to start? What caused it to end? Why should the ice have advanced and retreated four times?

The discovery of similar but older marks deepened the mystery. They showed that this was not the only ice age the earth had known. Still others occurred hundreds of millions of years ago. And the strange thing was that they held captive lands that we now know as tropical. Traces of these ancient glaciers have been found in Central Africa, Brazil, India, and Australia.

Over the years many scientists have advanced theories to explain the ice ages. To date no one theory has been proved right. No one has been accepted by all scientists. But perhaps the most widely held theory today is one developed by Lamont's

100

Maurice Ewing and his fellow scientist William L. Donn. They believe that two conditions set the stage of an ice age. The first is land in polar regions. The second is a warming of climate.

Like many other earth scientists, Ewing and Donn believe that in times past the earth's crust has shifted, sliding over the mantle. The cause of the shift is unknown. Ewing believes it resulted from convection in the mantle. Some other scientists have suggested a great addition of weight to one part of the crust—for example, the growth of a mighty mountain range. The mountains would add a great weight to one side of the earth. And the great weight might cause the earth to heave in its spinning. If the earth heaved, the crust would shift until the earth's spinning was again in balance.

Whatever the cause, a shift of the crust would change the polar regions. Polar lands would be carried to warmer areas. Warm lands would be carried to the poles. And this seems the most likely explanation of why ice ages apparently occurred in tropical lands. That is, these lands have not always been tropical. Once they lay at or near the poles.

Ewing and Donn believe that the last shift of the earth's crust carried Antarctica to the South Pole and the Arctic Ocean to the North Pole.

Antarctica, of course, was surrounded by water. So glaciers that grew there simply broke off in the sea and floated away as icebergs. But from the Arctic region glaciers could creep out over North

America, Europe, and Asia. And that is just what they did in the Ice Age.

Ewing and Donn believe that the Arctic Ocean is the key to the Ice Age. As we see it today, it is a small and nearly landlocked ocean, most of it covered with ice in summer as well as winter. It is the only ocean that freezes over. And it freezes, much like a large lake, because it is nearly surrounded by land. In the cold of winter only a little warm water can get into it from the south.

This warm water comes from the Atlantic. It enters where the two oceans meet, at the opening between Greenland and Norway. However, the two oceans do not mix much here because the sea bottom rises like a giant door sill and keeps them apart. At present only a relatively small amount of water crosses the sill.

But suppose now that the climate warms a little. Melt-water from glaciers pours into the oceans and raises their levels high above the sill. The oceans mix much more than before. Cold water from the Arctic pushes into the big Atlantic while warm water from the Atlantic rushes into the small Arctic Ocean. The Arctic Ocean becomes much warmer. It no longer freezes in winter, but remains open water.

Winter winds sweeping over the open water pick up a huge amount of moisture. As the moisture-laden winds blow across cold Arctic land areas, great snows fall. The snows feed the glaciers, piling up and being packed into ice. And the growing glaciers

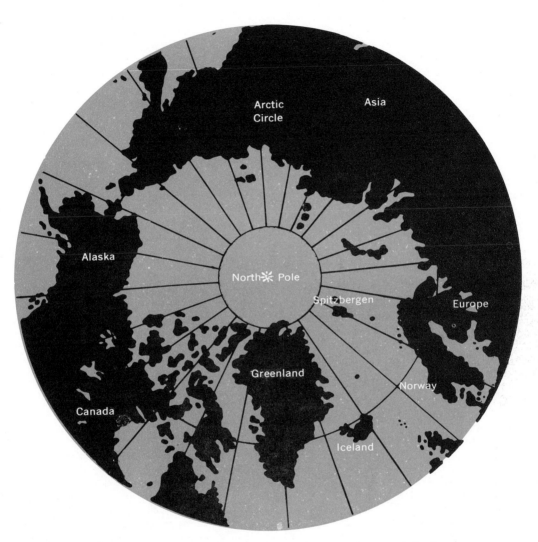

The small Arctic Ocean may be the key to the Ice Age. Because it is almost landlocked it freezes over, much as a large lake does.

On Baffin Island, off northern Canada, two glaciers form a great river of ice.

begin to flow. It is great snows, not great cold, that make glaciers grow.

As long as the Arctic Ocean remains open, the heavy snows continue and the glaciers grow, reaching out to capture lands to the south.

And there the glaciers are fed by still other snows. As moisture-bearing winds blow across the glacial ice, their moisture condenses and falls as snow.

But in time the great Arctic snows cease. A huge amount of water from the oceans is now locked up in ice, and ocean levels have dropped. The Atlantic and Arctic oceans no longer mix freely, and the Arctic again freezes over. Winds sweeping this ice pick up only a little moisture. Snowfalls are smaller, and more snow melts in summer than falls in winter.

Because the glaciers are no longer being fed, they begin to melt, drawing back to the Arctic. As they go on melting, ocean levels begin to rise. In time the Arctic and Atlantic again mix freely. The Arctic is again open in winter. And then the glaciers begin to grow.

The Ewing-Donn theory is the first that really accounts for the several advances and retreats of glaciers during the Ice Age. Their theory makes the growth and melting of glaciers part of a cycle. And this raises a very big question about the future: Are we nearing the time when glaciers will again grow?

IGY and other recent studies show that the climate has been warming up. In Iceland, Greenland, and Spitzbergen, temperatures have risen ten degrees in the past fifty years. Most glaciers are melting, and as melt-water pours off the land, ocean levels rise. The Arctic Ocean is warming at a rate that may make it ice-free in another forty years.

Scientists used to think that such warming marked the end of the Ice Age. They supposed that the time of ice had started with a cooling off of climate. And so warming of climate would melt the last traces of it. But the Ewing-Donn theory has caused many scientists to change their minds. They now think that glaciers may once more start to grow—if the warming continues.

But no one knows whether the warming will continue because no one knows what is causing it. And no one will know until the earth's climate is better understood.

Climate is produced by the working together of sun, air, and oceans. A change in any one of these three could produce a change in climate.

We know that the oceans carry seeds of change, but we do not know much more than that.

We know that the atmosphere acts as a greenhouse roof, and we know that events on the earth may affect it. For example, past periods of great volcanic eruptions may have added large amounts of carbon dioxide to the atmosphere. We may be doing the same thing ourselves today. The coal and oil burned in our modern world give off large amounts of carbon dioxide. The oceans absorb a good deal of carbon dioxide from the air, but they do not absorb

106

all of it. Extra carbon dioxide may strengthen the greenhouse effect and cause a warming of climate.

Then there is the sun. Changes in the sun's radiation would affect climate. And the sun's radiation does vary. At present it seems to be increasing, but scientists cannot yet tell whether this change is long-term or short-term. So they will continue to keep close watch on the sun for this and for a number of other reasons.

Watch
on
the
Sun

The sun that lights our sky is a large globe of gases, glowing with atomic fires. The fires were triggered in its core at the time the sun was born. Under conditions of tremendous pressure, nuclei of hydrogen atoms combined and turned into helium. This process, which is called nuclear fusion, still goes on today, and it produces great quantities of energy. Every second the sun changes 564 million tons of hydrogen into 560 million tons of helium. Four million tons of matter disappear. These are converted into energy, which is shot into the solar system as light, heat, and invisible radiation.

As stars go, ours is not very big—astronomers know of others a million times bigger. Even so, it contains enough hydrogen to go on shining for billions of years, in spite of the rate at which it burns up this gas.

The inside of the sun, where the nuclear reactions take place, is extremely hot. Astronomers think temperatures there are about 18 million degrees. They

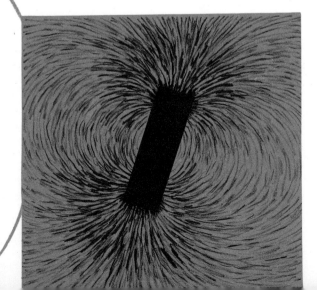

The earth acts as if it had a giant bar magnet inside. Just as a magnetic field forms around a bar magnet (this page), so does a field form around the earth (facing page). Radiations from the sun interact with this field.

109

also think that this part of the sun is kept in violent commotion by the energy being released.

Surrounding the central core is a thick layer made chiefly of hydrogen. This layer is much quieter. Energy from the core is carried through it to the surface by radiation.

A few thousand miles below the surface, the sun again begins to stir violently. Bubbles of hot gas, 200 to 1,000 miles in diameter, churn to the surface, climbing at about 1,000 miles an hour. These bubbles are what give the sun its grainy look in photographs.

When the bubbles burst, giant spikes of hot matter poke up from the sun's surface, reaching 2,000 to 5,000 miles into the sun's atmosphere.

The sun has two layers of atmosphere. The lower one is called the chromosphere. The upper one, called the corona, reaches millions of miles into space.

Since it is entirely gaseous, the sun does not have a solid surface like the earth's. Its apparent surface is more like a deck of angry, boiling clouds. And this surface is full of weather—of stormy disturbances.

The most violent disturbances on the sun show themselves as sunspots.

Sunspots appear as dark areas on the face of the sun, though they are not really dark but simply less bright than the surrounding areas. The smallest sunspots can hardly be told from the grainy bubbles. But the biggest ones are gigantic. Some have meas-

110

The sun's corona, photographed during a total eclipse.

ured 90,000 by 60,000 miles.

Groups of sunspots develop very quickly on the face of the sun. A group reaches its greatest size in about a week, then begins to decline. Big spots break up into smaller spots, then vanish. Sometimes it takes a few weeks for the whole group to disappear; sometimes the group lasts for a few months.

One of the strange things about sunspots is that they occur in cycles. On the average, periods of great sunspot activity occur once every eleven years. But sometimes there are long periods when hardly any sunspots appear. Almost none were observed between 1640 and 1716 or between 1796 and 1833. So far, no one has been able to explain either the cycles or the disappearances.

Scientists are fairly sure that sunspots are hurricane-like storms that spin and drift on the face of the sun. Their cause appears to be magnetic. Seemingly an unknown disturbance deep within the sun causes magnetism. The magnetism churns the sun's surface, making parts of it bulge and dim. These areas are sunspots. They are surrounded by

Sun spots, surrounded by bubbles of hot gas. This photograph was taken from a balloon 15 miles above the earth.

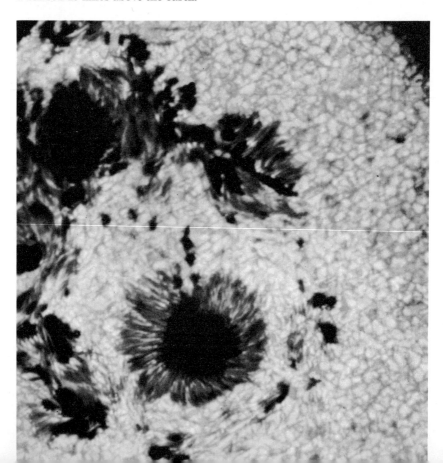

magnetic fields. And IGY studies showed that arching magnetic lines of force link pairs of sunspots.

Sunspots are accompanied by "prominences"—glowing jets, arches, loops, and clouds of gas. IGY scientists watched clouds of glowing gas float far up into the corona. They recorded a hydrogen jet 224,000 miles high that shot upward at 300 miles a second and lasted several days.

Solar flares are even more violent. Flares are brilliant bursts of extra-hot gas that break out of the sun near sunspots and shoot into space at speeds as great as 300,000 miles an hour. The flares hurl huge quantities of gases into space.

Our sun is normally an active star. But during sunspot periods it becomes extraordinarily active, and so the IGY was timed to coincide with such a period. It gave scientists a chance to study the sun at its most active.

During the IGY, scientists kept the sun under continuous observation. As the sky darkened and the sun slid from view in one part of the world, other observatories had already taken up the watch. During every minute of those 18 months, the sun was photographed. Giant radio telescopes reported its restless flickerings. The electronic and photographic eyes of rockets gave scientists their first clear view of the sun—as seen without the interference of the earth's atmosphere.

The purpose of this close watch on the sun was to observe, measure, and record its activities. And

113

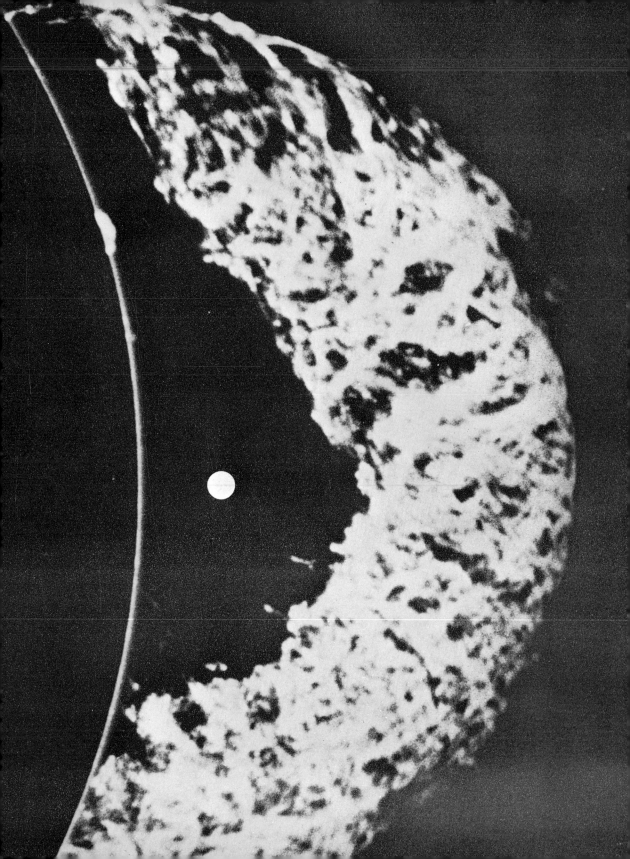

though the sun's mysteries are far from solved, scientists took a number of giant steps forward. They learned much about what happens on the sun. And they learned about the ways its radiation affects the earth.

The sun sends forth many kinds of radiation. Some provide our heat and light. Others have very different effects on the earth, which scientists are just beginning to discover and understand. These effects occur when radiation from the sun strikes the two barriers that surround the earth.

One of these barriers is the atmosphere. You have already read about some of the things that happen with the sun's rays there.

The second barrier is the earth's magnetic field.

Something within the earth makes our planet act like a giant bar magnet. As you know, a bar magnet has two ends, or poles. The earth also has two magnetic poles—a magnetic north pole and a magnetic south pole. These are the poles toward which com-

An enormous solar prominence, believed to be the largest ever recorded. It was 400,000 miles long, moving outward from the sun at 400 miles per second. The small white circle indicates the relative size of the earth.

pass needles point. They lie near the geographic poles but not in exactly the same places.

Every magnet has what is called a magnetic field. The field is invisible, but you can demonstrate it by scattering iron filings near a bar magnet. The filings will position themselves along the lines of force that make up the magnet's field. The result looks something like the drawing on page 109, with the lines of force arching from one pole to the other.

The earth's magnetic field has the same shape.

No one knows exactly what magnetism is. But all magnetic fields arise from electric currents. If you run a current through a wire (or any other conductor), a magnetic field forms around it. It is also true that if you place a conductor in a changing magnetic field, current flows through it; this is called an induced current.

Some scientists think that these facts contain the explanation of the earth's magnetism. The magnetism, they say, originated in the outer core when the earth was very young. There churning metal created a small electric current. The current produced a small magnetic field. As molten metal moved through the field, currents were induced in it. And these currents gave the earth its present strong magnetic field.

Not all scientists agree with that theory. But all do agree that the earth acts like a giant bar magnet, creating a large magnetic field. And all agree that magnetism and electricity are closely related;

116

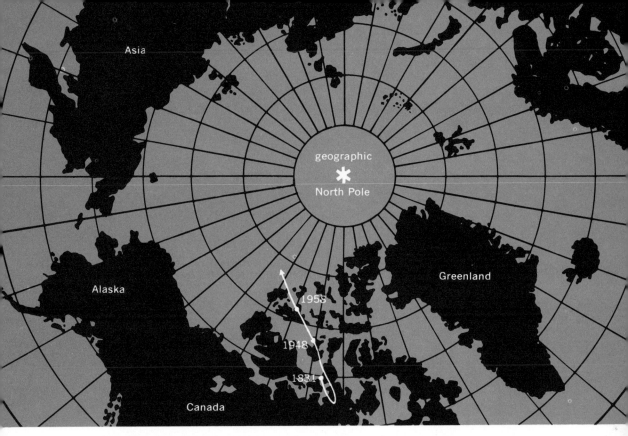

Asia

geographic
✳
North Pole

Greenland

Alaska

1953

1948

1831

Canada

A curious fact about the magnetic poles is that they wander, perhaps because of motion in the earth's core. This drawing shows how the north magnetic pole has moved in recent times.

each affects the other.

These facts are very important when it comes to understanding how the sun affects the earth. For many of the sun's radiations are made of electrically charged particles that interact with the earth's magnetic field.

117

Bullets
Belts
and
Borealis

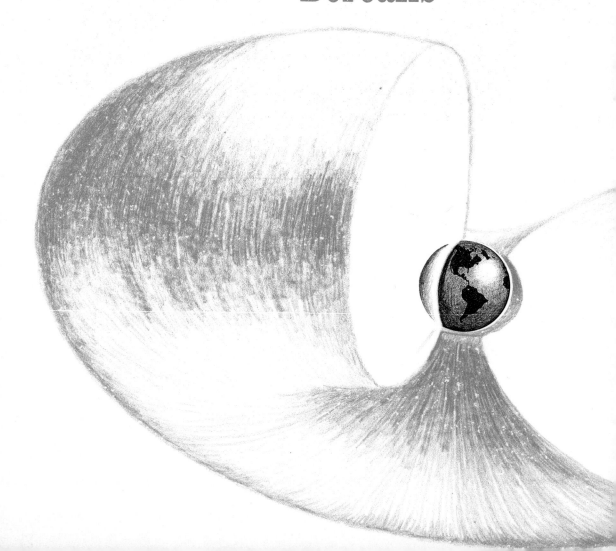

In science the most valuable discoveries are often the unexpected. These are the discoveries that fling open the door to new theories. These are the discoveries that advance man in his search to understand the laws of nature.

During the IGY, scientists made several such discoveries. One of the most important and surprising was made by a group that had set out not to discover the unknown but to study cosmic rays.

The Bullets

Every minute of the day and night, tiny cosmic bullets shower down on you and whizz through your body. These bullets are fragments of shattered atoms, called cosmic rays.

Most cosmic rays seem to come either from the

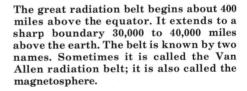

The great radiation belt begins about 400 miles above the equator. It extends to a sharp boundary 30,000 to 40,000 miles above the earth. The belt is known by two names. Sometimes it is called the Van Allen radiation belt; it is also called the magnetosphere.

stars or from space between the stars. However, their number increases after giant flares erupt on the sun; so it is likely that cosmic rays also come from our own star.

Cosmic rays begin as ordinary atoms traveling through space at tremendous speeds. They move almost at the speed of light—which is 186,000 miles a second. This speed means that each atom has a huge amount of energy.

Now, every atom is made up of a central nucleus surrounded by a shell of electrons. Cosmic rays move so fast that the electrons of each atom are stripped away. Cosmic rays approaching the earth have no electrons; they are simply nuclei. These are the primary cosmic rays.

As the primary rays near our planet, they meet the earth's magnetic field. They interact with it because they are electrically charged.

Some cosmic rays are bounced back into space by the magnetic field.

Others enter the earth's atmosphere by one of two routes. A few manage to push their way through the magnetic field. Others zoom in near the magnetic poles. Here the rays meet no magnetic resistance because they are traveling parallel to the lines of force.

As soon as they enter the atmosphere, cosmic rays begin to collide with air molecules and atoms.

Most of the rays are stopped by the atmosphere and never reach the ground. They plow through the atmosphere, knocking electrons off other atoms and leaving behind streams of charged particles.

Some primary rays score a direct hit on the nuclei of atoms in the air. Each time this happens there is an atomic explosion. The ray and the nucleus it strikes are shattered into particles. These particles are called secondary cosmic rays. They are the ones that shower down on the earth. Fortunately, they do not harm us.

Since very little is known about cosmic rays, they were made a field of study during the IGY. Scientists wanted to learn more about the rays themselves. And they wanted to know how dangerous primary rays might prove to space travelers, for these are far from harmless. They have the energy to penetrate spaceships and can kill cells in the human body.

Among the scientists studying cosmic rays was a team of U.S. physicists, led by James A. Van Allen. This was the group that made one of the IGY's most important and surprising discoveries.

The Belts

The Van Allen team discovered that the earth's magnetic field traps particles from the sun and from space. This magnetic trap creates an invisible belt of atomic particles that surrounds the earth except near the magnetic poles.

Some scientists had earlier suggested that the

121

James Van Allen, just before the launching of a balloon carrying instruments to measure cosmic rays.

earth's magnetic field trapped such particles. But the Van Allen group had not set out to test this theory. Its aim was to start the long job of counting primary cosmic rays. To do this, the team sent up Geiger counters in balloons, rockets, and satellites to measure the radiation.

Early measurements showed just what scientists had expected. Primary cosmic rays increased with altitude. The thinner the atmosphere was, the more cosmic rays the counters found.

But instruments in the U.S. satellite Explorer I told a peculiar story. The radiation count rose rapidly with altitude until the satellite was 1,500 miles above the earth. Here the counter reported either very low radiation or none at all.

A second counter sent up in Explorer III told the same story.

The team puzzled over these strange results. Then one of Van Allen's assistants, Carl McIlwain, suggested the solution. He reminded the others that a very high level of radiation can jam a counter, sending the reading to zero.

What they had found was not a lack of radiation but an area of very great radiation.

Further probes showed that a second area of high radiation lay beyond the first. At first scientists believed that these areas formed two distinct belts of atomic particles, which were named the Van Allen radiation belts. However, later satellite exploration seemed to show that the two belts are really one. These probes indicated that one vast belt of atomic particles spans each side of the earth, from magnetic pole to magnetic pole. The belt begins about 400 miles above the equator and extends to a sharp boundary 30,000 to 40,000 miles above the equator.

The earth's magnetic field apparently acts as a kind of giant umbrella. It keeps the radiation particles from reaching the earth, much as an umbrella keeps heavy snow off your head.

The outer region of the belt seems to be made of charged particles sent out in great clouds by solar flares. A day or two after the particles have left the sun, they dent the earth's magnetic field. Because of the field, their paths swerve. Instead of

123

continuing toward the earth, they whirl along the magnetic lines of force, shuttling back and forth between the two magnetic poles.

Scientists believe that the belt's inner region is made of strong primary cosmic rays. These particles apparently have enough energy to get through the outer magnetic field. But they are trapped by the inner field. Here they bounce back and forth between the magnetic poles, following the lines of force.

It will be many years before the Van Allen radiation belt is fully understood. But scientists are sure of two things.

One is that the particles in the belt present a very real danger to space travelers. They will be dangerous to manned satellites orbiting between 500 and 40,000 miles above the earth. They will be dangerous to manned interplanetary flights, unless the rockets are launched over the magnetic poles. Only there can they escape the belt.

The second thing known about the belt is that it plays a part in creating auroras, the strange night-sky lights that long mystified men.

Aurora Borealis

There are times when the night sky glows with colored lights. The lights take many shapes and forms. They may begin as a cloud, then spread into an enormous arc. They may fall in folds, like moving curtains drawn across the heavens. Brightness grows and dims. Huge rays stab the surrounding black of night. The sky glows pale yellow, pink, green, violet, blue, and red.

These lights are called auroras. Those that occur in the Northern Hemisphere are called aurora borealis. Those in the Southern Hemisphere are aurora australis. But since there are seldom many people around to see the aurora australis, scientists usually talk about the aurora borealis, or northern lights. These are the ones that scientists have been observing for hundreds of years.

In ancient times people found the lights terrifying and mysterious. They imagined they saw fiery dragons in the sky. They reported seeing battles and ships in the night sky. Sometimes they even thought the heavens were on fire.

Today we find the lights beautiful rather than terrifying. And we are beginning to find them somewhat less mysterious.

Quite some time ago, scientists decided that the auroras must be linked to the earth's magnetism. All auroras seemed to be centered on the magnetic poles. They also seemed to be somehow linked to sunspots and flares. Periods of sunspot activity were marked by many auroras.

In the 1890's, a Norwegian scientist named Kristian Birkeland carried out a spectacular experiment. He built a model of the earth and gave it a magnetic field. Then he fired electrons at it in a near vacuum like that of space. In his darkened labora-

125

After a giant solar flare, auroras seen on earth become brighter than usual.

tory, curtains of aurora-like lights ringed the model.

The experiment suggested that auroras were caused by particles from the sun. Drawn toward the magnetic poles, they rained upon the gases of the upper atmosphere and caused the lights.

Birkeland's work fascinated another Norwegian scientist, Carl Störmer. Störmer began to calculate, by mathematics, why the electrons behaved as they did. In 1907 he published his findings. Among other things, he showed how an electron could become trapped in the earth's magnetic field.

Recent research supports both Birkeland and Störmer.

Scientists now think that auroras are definitely caused by charged particles from the sun. The particles rush through the atmosphere at hundreds of miles a second and collide with air molecules and atoms. The result is a trail of atoms and molecules that are either excited or broken up. As the excited ones return to their normal state, they glow, giving off the lights that form auroras. The color of an aurora depends on the kind of atom or molecule that has been excited.

Everyday auroras seem to be caused by particles that have come directly from the sun. Being electrically charged, these particles are controlled by the earth's magnetic field. They spiral off toward the magnetic poles or enter directly there. That is why most auroras are seen in polar regions.

But there are times when a stupendous show of auroras goes on in the sky. The lights are bigger and brighter. And they are seen in areas far from the magnetic poles. These auroras always follow giant solar flares.

Scientists say such auroras are caused by solar particles that have earlier been trapped in the outer region of the Van Allen radiation belt. They remain trapped until they are shaken loose. Then they fall into the atmosphere, where they cause the brilliant auroras seen in many parts of the world.

What could shake particles out of the radiation belt? There seems to be only one answer: the great cloud of high-speed particles released by a solar flare. And the same cloud has much more drastic effects on the earth, for it is also the cause of a magnetic storm.

127

When
the
Sun
Storms

ionosphere

radio transmitter

The date was Sunday, February 9, 1958. At the Sacramento Peak Observatory in Sunspot, New Mexico, a staff member was watching the sun through an instrument called a monochromatic heliograph. It shows the sun's surface as gray. Against this gray background both bright and dark spots stand out clearly.

He was particularly interested in one group of sunspots. The spots covered three billion square miles on the face of the sun, and the region was obviously fuming and active. So far, on February 9, observers had counted seven solar flares there. More were expected.

At exactly 2:08 in the afternoon, the heliograph

Under normal conditions the ionosphere acts as a mirror for radio waves. But during a magnetic storm the mirror becomes "fogged" and radio communications are disrupted.

The Harvard Radio Astronomy Station, Fort Davis, Texas. It records bursts of radio noise during solar flares.

showed a giant flare of explosive brilliance.

Four minutes later the Harvard Radio Astronomy Station at Fort Davis, Texas, received a great burst of high-frequency radio noise. Such bursts of noise are a characteristic of big solar flares. When picked up on special receivers, they sound something like sausages sputtering in a frying pan.

The noise continued for a little less than two hours, ending just before 4 o'clock. At 4:02 the flare disappeared from the heliograph.

Some 28 hours later, the earth sailed into an enormous cloud of electrified gas, shot out by the giant flare. Scientists later estimated that the cloud must have been 46 million miles long and perhaps 23 million miles wide. When its nose arrived at the earth, its tail still reached halfway to the sun. The front part of the cloud was traveling at 870 miles a second, the tail at 435 miles a second.

Cloud and earth met at precisely 8:26 P.M. Eastern Standard Time, on February 10. That minute marked the start of one of the greatest magnetic storms on record.

Unlike a hurricane or blizzard, a magnetic storm cannot be seen or felt by people. It is not characterized by winds or cold or a darkening sky. It shows itself only in electric and magnetic effects. In our modern world these are staggering. Consider what happened on that night of February 10-11, 1958.

8:26 P.M.: The earth and cloud met. Needles on magnetic instruments in many parts of the world began to jiggle.

8:59 P.M.: Needles on magnetographs jumped—and in some cases went right off the page.

9 P.M.: Radio contact between North America and Europe suddenly faded out. A blood-red aurora spread across the skies of Canada and the northern United States.

9:01 P.M.: Service on transatlantic submarine telegraph cables was interrupted.

9:02 P.M.: Transatlantic telephone conversations began to fade, squeak, and squawk.

In the next few minutes, voltage in electric power lines was suddenly stepped up. Circuit breakers, designed to prevent overloading, began cutting off power. The Toronto area was plunged into blackness. In the northern United States lights flickered, dimmed, and sometimes went out.

In the hours that followed, radio contact was lost with South America and North Africa. Brilliant auroras were seen all over the dark half of the world. They were even seen near the equator, where these lights are almost unheard of.

It was a hectic night for several groups of people—for men who work with electric power, radio, telephones, and telegraphs. It was hectic for IGY scientists, who were busily recording every minute of the magnetic storm. But it was a terrifying night for the pilots of planes already in the air when the storm began. Most of them lost contact with the ground stations that normally guide and advise them.

132

On that night of February 10–11, some one hundred airplanes groped their way across the Atlantic. An Air Force pilot flew a passenger-laden plane over 2,000 miles of stormy seas and Antarctic ice without once being in radio contact with the ground.

In the hours after midnight, the storm began to die. The auroras continued. Scientists went on observing and measuring. But the worst was over. By morning radio contacts had again been made. Power lines and transatlantic cables were operating normally.

Twenty-four hours after its start almost all traces of the magnetic storm had vanished. At 10 A.M., February 12, it was declared officially over.

The effects of such a storm all stem from one thing: a meeting of the earth and a cloud of electrically charged particles from the sun. The charged particles interact with the earth's magnetic field and its atmosphere in various ways.

The particles set up gigantic electric currents in the outer atmosphere. Great sheets of electricity are generated in the sky, causing auroras. Giant currents surge through the earth and under the oceans, causing voltage to leap in electric cables and power lines. If the 1958 storm had been much bigger it could have done tremendous damage in its overloading of power lines and cables. Fortunately, the equipment was sturdy enough to handle the violent jump in current.

Radio contacts black out because of changes in the

ionosphere. As you know, the upper layer of the atmosphere is electrically charged. Under normal conditions this makes the ionosphere useful in beaming radio waves over long distances.

Since radio waves travel in straight lines, they cannot follow the earth's curved surface. So for long-distance communication, they are bounced off the

Telescope in the Azerbaijan region of the Soviet Union. It is used for studies of the sun's chromosphere.

ionosphere. The waves are beamed to the ionosphere from one place and reflected back to another. The ionosphere is often described as a mirror for radio waves.

During magnetic storms, the mirror becomes "fogged." It will no longer reflect radio signals, and that is why radio contacts are lost. No one knows exactly what happens to the ionosphere. But the barrage of extra-strong radiation from the sun somehow causes it to absorb radio waves rather than reflect them.

This breakdown in radio communication is of great importance in a world made small by rockets and jet planes. Military defense depends on orders flashed by radio. It depends on warnings from radar, and radar also uses the ionosphere.

All in all, many people in many fields have a great interest in learning more about what happens when the sun storms.

During the IGY, scientists collected masses of information about the ties between the sun and earth. But they are still far from understanding just what happens when the sun storms.

For example, a magnetic storm is always preceded by a flare on the sun. But flares—even big ones—are not always followed by magnetic storms. Some are and some aren't. At present there is no way of telling which flares will cause a storm and which won't. And so magnetic storms cannot be forecast.

To predict magnetic storms, scientists will have to

Among instruments for studying the sun is the orbiting solar observatory (OSO). Scientists plan an International Year of the Quiet Sun during 1964–65. The purpose: to compare the sun's behavior in a quiet period with observations made during the active period chosen for the IGY.

learn more about flares. And to learn more about flares they will have to learn more about sunspots. They need to know what causes sunspots and why they occur in cycles.

Then, too, there is reason to think that cycles of sunspots and flares affect the earth's weather and climate. Particles from flares seem to make the jet streams dip to an unusual degree. Dips in the jet streams affect the winds below and may create storms.

Some scientists think this explains why weather in our Southwest appears to be related to the sunspot cycle. Records show that when there are no sunspots, the Southwest tends to be dry and plagued by drought. During sunspot periods the droughts usually end. This may be simply coincidence. Or it could be explained by changes in the jet stream that flows above North America. When the jet stream is high, dry air hangs over the Southwest. When the jet stream dips, moist air is blown in.

This and other theories suggest that the sun may influence the earth in ways as yet undiscovered, that the earth has secrets still unguessed.

Yet today—with rockets and satellites and deep-sea drills, with electronic eyes and ears—scientists have the means of discovering the earth's big secrets. The new finds, the hints of clues that hang just beyond today's reach, suggest that a few things will be more exciting than future exploration of the planet Earth.

Index

141

The Author

Patricia Lauber is senior science editor of an encyclopedia for young people and the author of nearly thirty books, many of them about science. Random House has published her *All About the Ice Age* and *All About the Planets,* as well as two of her science books for younger readers—*The Story of Numbers* and *Your Body and How It Works. All About the Planet Earth* reflects her fascination with man's exploration of his home planet during the IGY. A graduate of Wellesley College, she lives in her native city of New York.

The Artist

Lee J. Ames, while artist in residence at Doubleday and Company, illustrated such science books as *Exploring the Sun* and *Man's Reach Into Space.* For Random House he has illustrated Raymond Holden's *All About Famous Scientific Expeditions* and a number of Landmark Books, including John Mason Brown's *Daniel Boone* and Samuel Hopkins Adams's *The Pony Express.* He lives in Floral Park, Long Island, N.Y., with his wife and their children, Jonathan David and Alison Sally.